THE STORE THAT HELPED BUILD CHICAGO

Gayle Soucek

Charleston | London

THE
History
PRESS

Published by The History Press
Charleston, SC 29403
www.historypress.net

Paperback edition first published 2010
Hardcover edition first published 2013

Manufactured in the United States

ISBN 978.1.62619.067.2

Library of Congress Cataloging-in-Publication Data
Soucek, Gayle.
Marshall Field's : the store that helped build Chicago / Gayle A. Soucek.
p. cm.
Includes bibliographical references.
ISBN 978-1-62619-067-2
1. Marshall Field's (Department store)--History. 2. Chicago (Ill.)--Economic conditions.
3. Retail trade--Illinois--Chicago--History. 4. Field, Marshall, 1834-1906. 5. Merchants--
Illinois--Chicago--Biography. 6. Chicago (Ill.)--Biography. I. Title.
HF5465.U64M377 2010
381'.1410977311--dc22
2010029560

CONTENTS

PREFACE TO THE NEW EDITION

Carve your name on hearts, not tombstones. A legacy is etched into the minds of others and the stories they share about you.
—Shannon L. Alder, author

It has been nearly three years since publication of the first edition of *Marshall Field's: The Store that Helped Build Chicago* and about seven years since the Marshall Field's name was wrenched from the Chicago landscape. Despite the time that has passed—or perhaps because of it—the collective hunger continues to grow for a memento of Chicago's treasured retail emporium.

As those who have lived in or traveled through the Windy City know, Marshall Field's was much more than a store. It was the embodiment of our city and its culture, a welcoming ambassador to the millions of wide-eyed tourists who visited and a comforting warm presence to the locals who grew up believing that Santa actually lived on State Street. Through war times and peace, economic busts and booms and floods and fires, the landmark store stood like a proud matron, unflappable and ageless.

But sadly, even an icon like Marshall Field's wasn't immune to the vagaries of corporate branding, and in 2006, the stores were renamed under the Macy's banner. Chicagoans felt as though they had lost a trusted friend and protested loudly. In fact, there is a continuing effort by various groups to encourage Macy's to restore the brand and return at least the State Street flagship to its former glory. It appears that an enthusiastic market awaits: a poll taken in late 2012 by Field's Fans Chicago showed that approximately four out of five Chicagoans wanted Field's to return, a number that has remained surprisingly consistent over past yearly surveys.

If I had any doubts about the accuracy of those numbers, they have long since been dispelled. Immediately after the first edition of this book hit the shelves, I was deluged with requests for book signings and speaking engagements, and the results were always the same: at every event, people approached me in droves with their own tender remembrances of the store. Many were former employees with tears in their eyes who described a valued career filled with respect and recognition. Although Marshall Field himself died in 1906, he left behind a legacy of honesty and loyalty that carried the company throughout its long reign as Chicago's favorite hometown store. Perhaps never before has a simple merchant become so inextricably entwined into the consciousness of an entire city.

As songstress Joni Mitchell once wrote, "You don't know what you've got 'til it's gone." That is certainly the case for those of us who thought that— sure as the sun rises over Lake Michigan, and sure as the Chicago Cubs will never shake the Billy Goat's Curse—Marshall Field's would always be there. The book that you are holding is my humble attempt to chronicle the great man's life and describe the enduring gifts that he left behind for the city he so loved. I hope it touches your heart as it did mine.

Gayle Soucek
February 2013

FOREWORD

I have always tried to make all my acts and commercial moves the result of definite consideration and sound judgment. I simply practiced honest, slow-growing business methods, and tried to back them with energy and a good system.

The School of the Art Institute of Chicago is my alma mater; I earned my BFA in art education there in 1968. I was thrilled to have Chicago (my place of birth) as my campus and the treasure-chest museum as my playpen. Also, with a straight face, I have claimed Marshall Field's as my alma mater—I had to work my way through school and did so in the phonograph record section on the ninth floor of one of my favorite places on the planet, at 111 North State Street. During that phase of my life, I also spent many an hour wandering the halls of the Field Museum, another favorite place. If contemplation, absorption and delight could extract physical material from its locus there would be nothing left of those institutions but the footprints. I carry my pieces still.

"Place" keeps coming up here. It is an amorphous word, just right for contemplating whatever it was that molded me into this person, writing these words in honor of the contribution made to my life by a long-dead man called Marshall Field. In an era of newly wealthy industrialists and entrepreneurs eager to demonstrate civic responsibility and cultural attainment in one stroke, he outdid himself. Funding museums or world expositions is a rather obvious way to see results, but Mr. Field, a merchant at heart, did not let it rest there.

He gave the lady what she wanted: a beautifully appointed, magnificently and completely stocked place in which to shop. Not only that, it was a safe and dignified place wherein to rest and refresh, to meet with friends and write to others, to dine. This place invited and welcomed, accommodated and provided. That was not all: it occasioned moments of awe and delight just about anywhere she looked.

In the 1960s, when some of the less-respected departments were clearly in need of realignment with Marshall Field standards, the lady was still welcomed and considered always right; she could return any merchandise on any pretext. I tied gold cord around many a white-wrapped gift; I hand-selected records or guitar picks or metronomes, I demonstrated, recommended and guided. We all did that sort of thing. The store provided "personal shoppers" who routinely traversed the store filling orders that came by phone or mail. However, no one was stationed at the entries to greet shoppers, who didn't need the input of a contrived gesture to feel glad they had just stepped into shopping heaven.

I indulged in Walnut Room lunches and teas, thoroughly acquainted myself with the stock of my favorite departments and returned a good portion of my paycheck whence it came, over the counter. Being a visual person, I relished the areas that struck me as well done and mourned the penal-gray desolation of the girls' clothing department. I rejoiced when they finally renovated the shoe department, giving a shot of high style to the midsection of the store. The arrival of Christmas was, of course, a joy to behold because it was still politically correct. The Great Tree was a riveting sight, as was the dense queue of visitors stoically waiting a turn to dine in its presence. I learned a lot with my eyes, and while I was not especially aware of it, I learned a lot about Doing Things Well and going the extra mile. It felt so good and adjusted my level of self-expectations upward.

That is what made Marshall Field's exceptional and compelling; it was the luscious rose to the bee. Yes, you could buy things there: belts and frying pans and door mats, Gucci and Chippendale and Jensen, knowing the store backed the quality and would even wrap it up in white and gold and deliver it as well. More importantly, you found pleasure and satisfaction in the process. This was a Place, a very fine one, where your needs were anticipated and met with a flourish, put together by a savvy man moved to enhance an otherwise mundane and wearying experience with beauty, quality, thoughtfulness and intelligence. His fellow merchants built similar stores, but none compared. The very name "Marshall Field's" is emotionally charged now; his flagship store is—or was—a precious oasis and landmark of grace and civility in our culture, not just for Chicago but also for the world.

Susan Greene
American Costume Studies
Alfred Station, NY 14803
March 2010

ACKNOWLEDGEMENTS

There is certainly no pleasure in idleness.

Writing a book of this nature is most definitely not a solitary pursuit. Long hours spent hunched over the computer, oblivious to everything except the gradually unfolding story appearing on the monitor, tend to take a toll on the author. Without the generous support and understanding of family, friends and co-workers, the task would be nearly incomprehensible.

With this in mind, I'd like to thank all those who contributed time, information, anecdotes, photos, memorabilia or moral support during this project. If I've missed anyone, please know I haven't forgotten your contribution, even if I have neglected to include your name here. Thanks to Jim McKay, Gloria Evenson and all the members of Field's Fans Chicago for everything you've provided, not the least of which have been friendship and support. Thanks to Susan Greene, Susan Pinto and Mike Russell, who were kind enough to share photos and remembrances, and to Shar Paul, Cathy Andorka, Lorena Lopez, Dan Sumiec and Barb Soberalski, who've always been in my corner.

And a special thanks goes to my ever-patient husband and live-in photography wiz, Peter Rimsa. Together, we make a great team.

Introduction

WHY MARSHALL FIELD'S MATTERS

To do the right thing, at the right time, in the right way; to do some things better than they were ever done before; to eliminate errors; to know both sides of the question; to be courteous; to be an example; to work for the love of work; to anticipate requirements; to develop resources; to recognize no impediments; to master circumstances; to act from reason rather than rule; to be satisfied with nothing short of perfection.

In these days of harshly lit "big box" superstores, mindless one-click online purchasing and vast dreary landscapes of endless strip malls, it can be difficult to explain why a single store chain, a lone brand name brought to the public perception over 150 years ago by a long-deceased merchant, should have any significance in our busy twenty-first-century lifestyles. After all, brands come and go, stores open and close and even once-cherished commercial giants drift into obscurity as the next generation of retailing or manufacturing brings the newest and the trendiest of the contenders to the forefront. Few remember or mourn once notable, now defunct department stores such as Wieboldt's, Jordan Marsh, McCrory, Britt's, Bamberger's or Carter Hawley Hale Stores. Why is Marshall Field's any different?

To answer that question is to touch upon the very essence of Chicago, the city that embraced the store. When young Marshall Field came to Chicago, he found an equally young city struggling to rise from the prairie and find its identity. The growth of the city and the growth of the store were symbiotic, each drawing the best from the other. Field was a leader who led by example, a man who not only spoke but lived by his priciples and set the bar for other entrepreneurs and civic leaders of the day. His philanthropy helped form the backbone of the city's culture, while his business acumen led commercial growth. "What would Field do?" became a mantra for other merchants who observed his methods and followed closely in line.

His generosity wasn't limited to showy displays of corporate beneficience; he was just as quick to supply mittens and coats to the poor errand boys who worked behind the scenes in his store when he observed their meager dress one cold day. Although frugal—some might say cheap—he never hesitated to use his wealth for the benefit of others.

The greatest good [a man] *can do is to cultivate himself in order that he may be of greater use to humanity.*

When Field died in 1906, his philosophy lived on in the store and the empire that he had built. Marshall Field & Company continued to help build Chicago and its outlying areas and created a legacy of civic commitment and customer satisfaction that lasted throughout another century and various corporate owners. When the Marshall Field name was retired in 2006 after the stores were purchased by Macy's, various protest groups coined phrases such as "Field's is Chicago" and "Field's: as Chicago as it gets." This wasn't just emotional hype.

Indeed, during the late 1990s and early 2000s, the flagship Marshall Field's store at 111 North State Street in Chicago was the third most visited tourist destination in the city, according to the Chicago Tourism and Convention Bureau. Busloads of wide-eyed visitors from across the globe came to Chicago to admire its natural beauty, enjoy its fine culture and shop at the world-reknowned store. Flight attendants at O'Hare Airport (second busiest in the nation) were quite used to seeing passengers carrying those familiar green bags stuffed with treasures for the folks back home. And Christmastime lunch at the famed Walnut Room restaurant was de rigueur for generations of Chicagoans. In fact, when talk first surfaced that the store's name might be changed by the new owners, few Chicagoans took it seriously, unable to believe that "Field's" and Chicago would ever be torn asunder.

Now, however, we live in a new era when corporate branding can change rapidly, sometimes capriciously. Chicago's own Sears Tower, once the world's tallest building, was named for a merchant peer of Field's. It is now the Willis Tower, named for a London-based insurance broker. Comiskey Park, the home of the Chicago White Sox baseball team since 1910, was moved and rebuilt in 1991 and, a few years later, renamed U.S. Cellular Field after the mobile communications company. The Rosemont Horizon, a huge sport and events arena in suburban Rosemont, became the Allstate Arena in 1999 when the insurance giant bought naming rights. Recent talk that the city's beloved and iconic Wrigley Field, home of the Chicago Cubs, might have its naming rights sold caused a near-meltdown in the press and among loyal fans. Life goes on, but most Chicagoans still refer to the tall building as the Sears Tower, the ballpark as Comiskey and the sports facility as the Horizon. Chicagoans are a loyal and stubborn lot who take a great deal of pride in things that are uniquely theirs. The loss of Marshall Field's was a painful lesson in brand loyalty that shook many residents from their complacency and created an awareness that civic identity shouldn't simply be sold to the highest bidder.

This book is intended to celebrate the life and philosophy of Chicago's greatest merchant and the continuing legacy he created. His generosity of both character and capital helped mold Chicago into the world-class city it is today and will live on in the institutions he helped to create. Throughout the text, you'll find quotes that illustrate the Field ideology. Unless otherwise attributed, all quotes are represented to be from Marshall Field himself. Of course, when researching events and hearsay from past centuries, it's sometimes difficult to pin down exact sources. In all cases, the author has attempted to use the most widely accepted or reliable source, but any discrepancies or errors are due to conflicting historical records and not from any lack of diligence or concern during the preparation of this manuscript. Mr. Field would demand no less.

Chapter I

From the Farm to the City

Making of a Merchant

Beware of a misfit occupation...I was always interested in the commercial side of life, and always thought I would be a merchant.

Chicago in 1856 was a city of contrasts. Obscene wealth mingled with desperate poverty. Gleaming white marble and limestone façades sprouted up from muddy, rutted streets. Plank highways roamed to the myriad frontier towns that were stubbornly setting down roots in the seemingly endless prairie, while the city itself appeared oddly restless and rootless. Towering grain elevators, dusty flour mills and bloody packinghouses sprang up to contain the massive wealth from the farms that dotted the prairie, while dirt-poor Irish and German immigrants struggled to provide a meager subsistence for their families. Nearly three thousand miles of iron rail spread like the spokes of a wheel from the city, connecting it to towns in the east and south, but traversing the narrow, swampy avenues from one end of the business district to the other created a challenge for residents. Each day, dozens of passenger trains from ten different trunk lines chugged into the upstart hamlet, disgorging a steady stream of eager pioneers ready to seek their fortune in the growing metropolis. Some came to get rich on their wits and intellect, others on their strength and brawn, toiling from dawn to dusk in soul-crushing labors.

Once a sleepy little fur-trading community on the shores of Lake Michigan, Chicago had much working in its favor to assist in its rapid growth. Situated at the mouth of the Chicago River on the southwestern edge of the third-largest Great Lake, it was an ideal port for ships from the east. Even during its earliest days, visionaries recognized the town's remarkable potential as a transportation hub, and they began to dream about a great canal that would allow barges filled with goods to travel from the Great Lakes, down the Mississippi River, all the way to the Gulf of Mexico. Finally, in 1848, the visions became reality as construction was completed on the ninety-six-mile-long Illinois and Michigan Canal that connected the Chicago River to the Illinois River.

This engineering marvel of the time allowed vessels to travel from Chicago through the canal to the Illinois River, which emptied into the mighty Mississippi. Sturdy paths on either side of the sixty-foot-wide canal were designed for mules to pull the provision-laden barges through the shallow channel until they reached the rivers. Because the mules needed to rest from their labors, towns grew up along the paths at appropriate distances, allowing the animals and their handlers to obtain food and shelter. Now, goods could be shipped from the East Coast, through the Great Lakes, through the new Port of Chicago, all the way down to New Orleans. The scrappy frontier town of Chicago was gaining quite a bit of notoriety out east as a place to be reckoned with, a city growing from the prairie at a phenomenal rate, representing all the promise that the West had to offer. In 1833, the population of Chicago was approximately 300; by 1860, that number had grown to 110,000.

Of course, as the people came, the need for goods and services increased. Lake Street, which runs parallel and close to the Chicago River, became known as "the street of merchants." Unfortunately, the slow-moving Chicago River was a repository for sewage and dead animals, and residents of the day often covered their faces with handkerchiefs to block the stench as they hurried through the swampy mud to visit one of the new emporiums. Slaughterhouses added their offal to the mix, and the vile smells of animal putrefaction mingled with the odor of human waste sometimes caused residents to gag and retch. These noxious odors, known as "miasmas," were often blamed for disease, but in reality it was the lack of sanitation and understanding of germ theory that caused frequent outbreaks of cholera, scarlet fever and typhoid.

Wooden sidewalks helped the residents avoid some of the muck, but the smells, smog and dust from horses and wagons still permeated the air, especially during the broiling hot summer months. Chicago was, after all, built on marshy swampland, and the rapid population growth and overcrowding overwhelmed any attempts at sanitation. Diseases swept through in periodic waves, leaving massive death tolls in their wake.

In spite of these challenges, Chicago was destined to become a world-class city, and it required world-class goods and services. Women of the time clamored for luxurious silks and laces like those in Parisian fashion houses. Even the plain farm wives of the nearby prairies yearned to introduce a bit of fancy into their hardscrabble lives. The boom also brought lawyers, financiers, railroad men and industry magnates from the east and south, cash in hand, all looking to lay claim to a piece of the rapidly growing western outpost. And where the cash went, the merchants soon followed.

Portrait of Marshall Field, age twenty-four.

One of these arriving merchants was twenty-one-year-old Marshall Field, a farmer's son from Conway, Massachusetts. Marshall was born on August 18, 1835, the fourth of eight children born to John "Jack" and Fidelia Nash Field. His birth year is most frequently listed in biographies as 1834, but his gravestone shows his year of birth as 1835, and Field himself once mentioned 1835 in an early interview. The Field family was descended from Puritans who had migrated to New England en masse in the mid-1600s to develop their own community, free from what they considered an unwelcome tolerance toward Catholicism in the Church of England. Puritans believed in leading a simple, frugal, "Godly" life and placed a strong emphasis on moral values and family life. The Puritans of New England also placed a high value on education, for without literacy one could not read or understand the scriptures or the capital laws of the new country. In fact, by the mid-seventeenth century, almost all New England states had laws in place requiring education of children.

The Field family was no exception, and Marshall and his siblings were well educated and imbued with strong moral character at home. Marshall did attend school up through high school but decided to forego college and strike out toward his dream of becoming a man of business. In his later years, he spoke with some disdain on the subject of higher education: "Every person has two educations—the one he receives from others, and one, more important, that he gives himself…Often when he comes out of college the young man is unfitted by this good time to buckle down to hard work, and the result is a failure to grasp opportunities that would have opened the way for a successful career."

Marshall knew from an early age that he had no interest in following his father into a backbreaking life of farming. He once told an interviewer that he was "determined not to remain poor" and knew that his calling would be in merchant trade. His parents were supportive of his dreams, and when he turned sixteen, they sent him to nearby Pittsfield in the employ of a fellow Congregationalist, Deacon Henry G. Davis, who owned a small dry goods store in the town.

Marshall immediately applied himself to the job in a focused and intense manner. He slept in a small room above the store and awakened at dawn to sweep, clean and arrange inventory. The hours were long—ten hours or more a day, six days a week. In his precious off hours, he declined the social activities of his peers and instead studied publications of the time such as *Hunt's Merchant's Magazine* and *Godey's Lady's Book* in order to better understand the trade. And young Marshall did become a hit with the ladies. His quiet and exceedingly polite demeanor and his superb listening skills endeared him to many. He asked the proper questions and spent the time necessary to make sure that all customers left with exactly what they needed. He worked diligently to memorize product features and prices so that he could discuss any item in the store with confidence and authority.

After nearly five years in Pittsfield spent honing his skills, Marshall ached to strike out on his own. The opportunities in small-town New England were limited, but merchant magazines wrote gushing stories about the nearly limitless opportunities in the West, especially in the boomtown of Chicago. Marshall's older brother, Joseph, encouraged him to take the leap. In fact, Joseph was heading to Chicago himself and would help pave the way for his younger brother. When Deacon Davis heard of the plan, he immediately offered Marshall a partnership in the Pittsfield store in an effort to entice him to stay, but Marshall politely declined—it was time to pursue his dreams. So, in the spring of 1856, an eager and optimistic twenty-one-year-old Field stepped off a Michigan Central train into the bustle and commotion of the new frontier.

Chicago must have been quite a shock for Marshall after growing up in a small and relatively sedate eastern community. Here, throngs of people, horses and wagons clogged the streets with a never-ending cacophony of noise and dust. New construction was going up everywhere, and dry goods stores of a size never before imagined lined Lake Street. And one of the most impressive was a retail emporium named P. Palmer & Company, run by a "Yankee trader" like Field himself.

Potter Palmer had arrived in Chicago in 1852 after owning a dry goods store in Oneida, New York. He was a twenty-six-year-old Quaker, with almost eight years of experience as a merchant under his belt, when he came to Chicago seeking greater opportunities. Palmer, like Field, had an intuitive understanding of the lady shopper. With a new movement called "feminism" afoot, it only made sense that the female shopper would soon be a significant factor in a merchant's success. Early dry goods stores were rough establishments that sometimes doubled as taverns, and a proper lady would hurry in to make her necessary purchases and leave promptly. Palmer sought to make his new Chicago store different. He purchased a fine assortment of ladies' goods from as far away as Paris and displayed them in a clean and attractive manner. Large, enticing window displays, almost unheard of at the time, beckoned the shoppers inside. Once the shoppers were there, the attentive clerks would show off the goods and answer any questions the ladies might have. Although most of his wares were out of the range of what the poor immigrants and farm wives could afford, he made sure that they, too, were treated with respect and allowed to browse as long as they wished. This courtesy ensured that they would return to him when they did indeed have the means to make a purchase.

One of Potter's most outrageous policies made him the laughingstock of other merchants. He actually allowed some of his better clients to take home merchandise "on approval." The lady could choose a fine silk shawl, for example, with the invoice directed to her husband. If the husband did not approve, the item could be returned to the store without questions. This return policy made his store very popular with the ladies, despite the derision of his peers. Soon, other merchants would grudgingly begin to follow his lead in order to remain competitive. By the time Marshall Field arrived on the Chicago scene in 1856, P. Palmer & Company was one of the premier retail establishments in town.

It wasn't Palmer's firm, however, that first benefited from Field's salesmanship and attention to detail; it was the competitive Cooley, Wadsworth & Company, a large Chicago wholesaler with a small retail operation. Marshall's brother Joseph was acquainted with the elder Cooley and accompanied Marshall on his interview. Cooley was unconvinced by the young man's promise but eventually relented to Joseph's pleading and offered Marshall a retail clerk position with a salary of $400 per year. Field jumped at the opportunity and was determined to prove his worth. While the other young clerks attended dances and social gatherings on their off time, Marshall memorized prices and inventory, just as he had at Deacon Davis's store. When he wasn't busy selling, he unloaded merchandise and moved freight. It didn't take long for Cooley to realize he had indeed made a wise decision by hiring the hardworking youth.

Shortly after Field started with the firm, Wadsworth retired, and a junior partner named John V. Farwell stepped in to form a new partnership named Cooley, Farwell & Company. Wadsworth remained a "silent partner" for a few years, leaving some capital in the business but distancing himself from the daily operations. Field's industriousness had also caught the attention of Farwell, who noted that Marshall "had the merchant's instinct" and was quickly favored by the lady shoppers. Even though he was a mere junior clerk, many of the wealthy women who frequented the store asked to deal with the young Mr. Field, who listened to them with rapt attention and patiently answered all their questions. Farwell believed this natural talent for salesmanship would serve the firm well in its wholesale division and suggested to Cooley that Marshall be promoted to an outside sales position. And so, with a stack of calling cards and a satchel full of samples, Marshall headed out to the sleepy farm towns and small cities to introduce a new world of available goods.

In the past, small-town general store proprietors would need to make a laborious trek by horse and wagon to trading centers to acquire goods to furnish their stores. Now, however, the traveling salesmen came to visit with samples and catalogues. The orders were then shipped to the store, sometimes by wagon but increasingly by the various railroad lines that were spreading across the land. Although most merchants had dealt on a cash-only basis, forward-thinking firms such as P. Palmer and Cooley & Farwell judiciously offered credit to their prime customers. Cooley & Farwell had employed a young credit manager for that very purpose: Levi Z. Leiter.

Levi was born of Calvinistic Dutch heritage in Leitersburg, Maryland, in a town founded by his grandfather Abraham. He was the same age as Field and shared his enthusiasm for the mercantile life. Levi began his business career at a small dry goods store in his hometown and later at another establishment in Springfield, Ohio, before moving to Chicago in 1854. His skill at bookkeeping and shrewd aptitude for wise credit decisions made him a valuable addition to Cooley & Wadsworth, and by late 1856 he had reached

Postcard showing future site of Marshall Field's, circa 1839.

the enviable position of head accountant, with the unheard-of salary of $2,500 per year. Marshall and Levi enjoyed a mutual respect and spent much time exchanging ideas and dreaming of better ways to grow the business.

Those ideas would quickly be brought to the test in 1857, when the country lapsed into a financial panic. It began with the failure of Ohio Life Insurance and Trust Company and quickly spread to a nationwide run on banks as investors pulled their funds. About five thousand businesses failed in a year, including railroads and banks. Grain prices plummeted, leading to severe hardship in the agricultural core of the United States. The panic spread to Europe, the Far East and South America in what was probably the first example of the developing global economy. Stock prices dropped precipitously, and as unemployment rose, riots broke out in some cities.

Even the boom town of Chicago was not immune to the financial collapse. Cooley & Farwell had just finished construction on a spacious and modern store on Wabash Avenue, complete with ultra-modern steam elevators and all the trappings expected in such a prestigious emporium, when the panic hit. The partners borrowed heavily from family and friends to avert backruptcy and remain afloat, even taking bushels of grain and furs in payment from struggling customers. Many of their competitors were not so lucky, and "ceasing business" and "distress" sales became the norm. Only one other merchant seemed to carry on business as usual, and that was Potter Palmer. Although he ceased his wholesale business, Palmer chose that time to move to a larger and more beautiful store on Lake Street and continued to cut his prices to undersell the competition. He purchased goods at rock-bottom prices from panicked wholesalers on the East Coast and heavily advertised his low prices. While other merchants made deep cuts in their inventory, only Palmer continued to buy new goods and expand his business.

Luckily, the Panic of 1857 was short-lived, and by 1858, things were looking up. Some merchants who had declared "quitting business" sales managed to survive after all, including T.B. Carter and W.M. Ross, but P. Palmer & Company came out of the depression as the undisputed leader in Chicago retail trade. None of this was lost on Field. He had taken careful note of each competitor's strategy, and he analyzed what had worked and what hadn't. Around this time, Cooley & Farwell were in a position to add a new junior partner, and Marshall was the obvious choice. Although Field had no significant capital to contribute, he was given a salary of $3,000 a year and complete control of sales and credits. Meanwhile, Cooley moved to New York to handle purchasing for the firm.

Just about a year later, however, the senior partners decided to buy out Wadsworth completely and now needed some more capital and another full partner. They offered it to Field for the sum of $15,000. By this time, Marshall had about $4,000 in savings, and could borrow another $1,000 from his family, but was still $10,000 short of realizing his dream. The elder Cooley, who had once doubted young Field's potential, now fully recognized his junior partner's remarkable talents and offered to loan him $10,000 at 6 percent interest, to be paid back gradually from Field's share of the profits.

By late 1858, Palmer was ready to expand once more, this time leasing a stunning new marble-fronted five-story building just one block east from his former location. This "marble palace" had originally been intended to house at least three firms, but Palmer leased it all and cut archways throughout the first-floor walls to create a huge display showroom, the largest in the West. He also rekindled his wholesale trade, filling large warehouses with products of every description. With Cooley in New York doing purchasing, Palmer also opened a New York buying office and began to send buyers to Europe. Palmer had realized that by cutting out the middleman importers, he could buy and ultimately sell at prices lower than his competitors.

Once again, however, the nation's economy was rocked by crisis: the beginning of the Civil War in 1861. Due to general fears and the uncertainty of trade, especially the availability of southern cotton, a rapidly escalating period of inflation hit the country. The value of the dollar was down, while the price of goods skyrocketed. Most merchants cut back on purchases, fearing an inevitable collapse and deflation, but Palmer continued to buy. During this time, Cooley wrote to Field from New York: "[Palmer has] been buying goods at high prices…I stopped buying and he is in no better shape than we are…I *may be* wrong." Indeed, Palmer's antics turned into a profitable gamble. Prices had nearly doubled by the time the war was ending in 1865, and Palmer was one of the few that had a strong enough inventory throughout the war years to appease the escalating demand.

By this time, Cooley's health was failing, and he decided to leave the business. Field and Farwell, although quite a successful team, were not particularly fond of each other on a personal level. The easygoing Farwell found Field too rigid and puritanical, and Field seemed to feel stifled by his cautious partner. Marshall had long maintained a friendship with William McCormick, whose brother Cyrus had invented the mechanical reaper that was the early foundation for International Harvester Corp. Field turned to the brothers for help, desperately hoping to borrow enough capital to buy out Farwell. Although William was interested, Cyrus was busy and distracted and didn't act upon the opportunity in time. Thus, out of necessity the new firm of Farwell, Field & Company was born.

The partners quickly decided to add a junior partner, and head accountant Levi Leiter immediately jumped at the opportunity. With greater prosperity and a bright future ahead, Field impetuously married Nannie Douglas Scott in 1863. She later bore him two children, Marshall Jr. in 1868 and Ethel in 1873, but the marriage was not a happy one. Field was engrossed in his business pursuits, and the new Mrs. Field spent a great deal of time in Europe with the children. With Farwell and Leiter handling things in Chicago, Field decided to travel back to New York and take over the buying that Cooley had done. National Bank Acts in 1863 and 1864 served to stabilize currency and stimulate trade, and Field began an aggressive buying campaign, filling warehouses and stockrooms to their limits. Within months, the *Chicago Tribune* named Farwell & Field the number one wholesale house in the city. However, the animosity between the principals continued to grow.

In many ways, Farwell was simply tired of the dry goods business. He wrote Cooley that he wanted to get out and invest his money in real estate, "before things go into the old Channels again, with competition on every corner." Field, for his part, chafed at Farwell's caution and wanted to grow the business like that of their chief rival, Potter Palmer. Levi also wanted to leave and join forces with Field, but the two of them together only had access to a combined capital of a little more than $300,000, not nearly enough to build a competitive firm from scratch. Marshall once again approached the McCormicks, who once again dawdled at making a decision. However, someone else had heard Field's plea through whispered conversations on the street and in exclusive clubs: none other than Potter Palmer.

Palmer, at thirty-eight, was a millionaire many times over, not just from his dry goods business but also from well thought out investments in real estate. Unfortunately, his hard-driven lifestyle had taken a toll on his health, and his doctor urged him to slow down. Potter had been watching the competitive young Field for many years and had high regard for his business acumen. He also knew and respected Levi Leiter and considered the two men a formidable team. In December 1864, Palmer approached them with an offer almost too good to be true: he would sell Field and Leiter his business, lock stock and barrel, for 20 percent below the inventory value, provided they accept his brother, Milton Palmer, as a junior partner. Potter was no fool; he realized that the money that Field and Leiter possessed would not be sufficient to capitalize the firm, so he agreed to remain a silent partner and leave $330,000 in the business until such time the new owners could afford to buy him out. Field was required to put up $250,000 and Leiter $120,000. Milton would also contribute $50,000, bringing the total capitalized value to $750,000. The new firm was named Field, Palmer, and Leiter, with the "Palmer" referring to Milton, not Potter, who wished to remain removed from the day-to-day operations.

And so, just barely into their thirties, Marshall and Levi found themselves the senior partners of the West's largest and most prestigious dry goods house. In January 1865, they began to advertise the new firm as "successors to P. Palmer," while Potter himself sailed off to Europe for a vacation planned to last three years. Their joy, however, was premature. In April, just four months after the birth of the new firm, the Confederacy collapsed, bringing the Civil War to an abrupt halt. Suddenly, the inflated wartime prices dropped precipitously, sending the economy into another freefall. Northern merchants, including Field and Leiter, found themselves with warehouses bulging with merchandise that was worth less than they had paid for it. They began to run panic sales to undercut the competition and maintain sales volume, but it was clear the fledgling firm couldn't survive for long at the rate they were bleeding red ink. Frantic, they begged for Potter to return and take back the firm.

Potter did return, but mostly to shore up their confidence and help with strategy. As usual, the unflappable Potter advised them to continue full steam ahead: "This day of low prices won't last. Take my advice. Go into the market and buy all you can…you buy and think faster than the fellow down the street, and you'll come out alright!" He bought back $25,000 of Field's investment in order to infuse the firm with a little more cash and instructed them to carry on. Encouraged, Field and Leiter did just that. Field spent much of his time in New York, buying merchandise as per Palmer's admonishment. In addition, they began to loosen their credit restrictions a bit, just at a time when other wholesalers were tightening theirs. It was a risky and stressful move for the fiscally conservative Leiter, but the partners reasoned that helping keep their best clients afloat during the troubling times would pay off down the road. Their instincts were correct; as the economy recovered, those who had been granted a little respite gratefully returned in full force to the firm that had carried them. Field and Leiter's reputation as honest, ethical and fair businessmen was rock solid, and business once again began to boom.

By the time the year ended, despite its rocky start, the new partners had realized $8 million in gross sales, with a bottom-line profit of over $300,000. By the end of their second year, they were able to buy out the Palmers, and on January 1, 1867, the firm once again required a fresh set of stationery, inscribed with the new name of Field, Leiter & Company. The future certainly looked bright indeed for the young merchants.

Chapter 2

GROWTH AND REBIRTH

Field, Leiter & Company

Merit did not have to wait for dead men's shoes in a growing town…Good qualities were usually promptly discovered, and men were pushed forward rapidly…Everything was coming this way [to Chicago]…*and the man who learned the quickest fared the best.*

Field and Leiter were certainly fast learners. Having weathered a severe financial crisis during their first year of operation, they'd quickly identified the strengths and weaknesses of the trade, as well as the country itself, and had surrounded themselves with some of the brightest associates in the city. Field was a skilled judge of character, and only those who passed his scrutiny joined their ranks. In fact, the firm had a strict policy against hiring employees who "gambled or used intoxicants to excess, or whose conduct outside the store was in any way below the Field standard." By holding their employees to the strict standard of character and ethics displayed by the principals, the partners were able to establish a reputation so valuable that it became a standard by which other businesses were judged.

Some of the "bright young men" who made up the business were employees of Potter Palmer, but others were culled from competitors or followed Field from his days at Cooley & Farwell. Henry Willing had served as a top salesman at Field's competitor T.B. Carter, and also at Cooley & Farwell, before he was hired to head the store's popular calico section.

By 1867, he was allowed a small partnership interest in the firm and had expanded his duties to wholesale merchandising. Lorenzo Woodhouse was a young salesman at Farwell's establishment, and when he joined Field & Leiter, he quickly proved his buying instincts were so good that he was trusted to run the New York buying office, allowing Field to return to Chicago full time. Woodhouse helped develop many of the merchandising policies that served the store in future years.

Harlow Higinbotham, another former Cooley & Farwell employee, served in the Mercantile Battery during the Civil War and returned to serve as assistant to Levi Leiter. Higinbotham used his uncanny ability for astute credit decisions to run the day-to-day operations of the credit department, allowing Leiter the freedom to work on broader policies and the larger financial picture. Harlow garnered a small partnership share in 1879 and served the company faithfully until his retirement in 1900.

Perhaps one of the most novel positions in the firm was also one of the most important: Thomas Templeton, a "master mathematician," applied his genius with numbers to gather and analyze statistics, reports and sales figures, providing invaluable data that allowed the partners to react intelligently and appropriately to changes in the market. For example, a financial downturn from a flood or crop failure in another area of the country might eventually affect the company's wholesale division, but with Templeton's precise analysis and predictive ability, Field & Leiter could sidestep these bumps with near impunity. Financial forecasting was a new science, but Field was, once again, at the forefront, and Templeton was also rewarded with a small partnership share.

In the sales department, Field's brothers Henry and Joseph joined the firm, along with a smart young salesman named Aaron Montgomery Ward. Ward soon realized that eliminating the middleman and purchasing products through the U.S. mail might better serve his customers in remote rural towns. He left Field & Leiter's employ in 1872 to open his own mail-order house, which grew to sales of over $40 million a year by his death in 1913.

It was this nurturing of abilities that contributed strongly to Field's success. He believed in hiring the best, patiently grooming their innate skills and rewarding them accordingly. The cream of the crop were promoted quickly and given a share of the firm, but even the average employee was treated with dignity and respect and could depend on the company to look out for his best interests. During the early 1870s, when the combined retail and wholesale payroll included more than one thousand employees, Field was known to walk through the buildings, personally greeting each employee, shaking hands and asking solicitous questions about the individual's family. It's been said that he had a near photographic memory of faces and names and never failed to remember an employee, customer or business associate.

It wasn't just bright young men who enjoyed the mentorship of the master retailer. Field was one of the first merchants to hire promising young saleswomen. He realized that lady shoppers might be embarrassed to purchase some necessities, such as undergarments or potions, from male associates. By staffing certain departments with female clerks, a lady wouldn't be made to feel uncomfortable when shopping for "unmentionables." And shop they did. With a veritable smorgasbord of fine merchandise, eye-catching displays, helpful and understanding clerks, fair prices and a liberal return policy, Field and Leiter left other merchants in the dust. Field, it seemed, had accomplished something no man had ever done before: he understood the feminine psyche.

There's a famous and oft-told story that illustrates Field's attitude toward his customers. It's said that as he walked through his retail palace one day, he heard a clerk arguing loudly with a female shopper. Field quickly stepped over and demanded to know what was happening. "I'm settling a complaint," explained the hapless clerk. Mr. Field fixed him with a steely blue-eyed glare and said, "No you're not! *Give the lady what she wants!*" Those six words have been a catchphrase for the Field's empire up through the current day and precisely sum up his customer-centric style.

Field also had an uncanny understanding of lifestyle and culture during his time. He anticipated the needs of his customers in ways that few of his contemporaries ever did. He knew exactly which sturdy and practical notions would appeal to the farm and frontier communities of his wholesale customers and which expensive and perhaps frivolous items would catch the fancy of the wealthy city dwellers. Rather than catering to just the carriage trade, as some had tried before, Field filled his vast inventory with items for every socioeconomic group. Although the store had a reputation as high-end, it was never pretentious. In fact, Field was quick to warn his staff that they must never judge customers upon their dress, and they were obliged to treat everyone with the same level of respect and courtesy. It was a store where a lady could purchase a ridiculously extravagant Persian cashmere shawl for $1,200 or a yard of colorful calico for less than a dime and still receive unerringly superior service. The only requirement for merchandise was that it was the best quality of its type and was advertised honestly.

I made it a point that all goods should be exactly what they were represented to be. It was a rule of the house that an exact scrutiny of the quality of all goods purchased should be maintained, and that nothing was to induce the house to place upon the market any line of goods at a shade of variation from their real value. Every article sold must be regarded as warranted, and every purchaser must be enabled to feel secure.

At a time when competitors were stamping their invoices "absolutely no returns," Field's generous and unquestioning return policy encouraged both retail and wholesale customers to buy with confidence. He also continued Palmer's practice of "one price" pricing. Other merchants might pad the price a bit when a customer in fancy dress showed interest in an article or haggle to lower the price if it suited them. Field would have none of that. His prices were determined to give the best possible value to his customers while still allowing the firm to make a necessary profit.

In fact, everything that Field did was based on absolute honesty and integrity. During that era, "sharks" and speculators invaded the business districts, throwing open businesses that quickly peaked and disappeared, leaving a trail of empty-handed creditors in their wake. Field and Leiter instead dealt strictly on the strength of character, both their own and that of their customers. Perhaps as a result of his Puritanical upbringing, Field believed that paying one's honest debts was a man's first duty. "No man is good who does not pay his debts, no matter how wealthy he may be," said Field, and the business adhered strictly to that philosophy. When the great Chicago fire of 1871 swept through the business district, destroying everything in its path, some suppliers sent letters of sympathy, offering extended terms or price settlements to their Chicago clients. Field & Leiter graciously declined the generous gestures, telling creditors that they would pay "100% on the dollar" and within agreed terms.

Of course, the partners expected the same of their customers. Although they were willing to work with valuable customers to extend terms and keep them afloat during a rough patch, and Field personally was known to quietly help finance the occasional fledgling businessman, nothing raised their ire faster than a cheat or a deadbeat. There are several accounts of Leiter's less than gentle treatment of those who misrepresented their ability or willingness to pay. According to a *Chicago Tribune* article, he once shouted, "You promised it and you did not do it! Get out or I will have the porter throw you out!" at one delinquent client. Field publicly scoffed at wholesalers

Portrait of Levi Leiter.

who offered long payment terms, believing it was a form of dishonesty. After all, the expense of conducting business in that manner had to be hidden somewhere, and it was usually borne in higher prices to the customer. He once noted that some of his competitors "seem to think they are selling time instead of dry goods."

Because of their tight control of credit and burgeoning sales, Field & Leiter had the ability to forecast accurately, buy in huge volume and pay on close terms. Bankers, manufacturers and importers fell over themselves to win and maintain the firm's confidence. As early as 1870, the partners were able to buy the entire output of large factories, making them one of the most desired customers of the era. In this manner, Field and Leiter actually helped create a business and banking culture in Chicago that was more ethical than had previously existed in the town's rowdy frontier past. Their reputation for honesty, integrity and rapid and reliable payment spread far beyond Chicago, however, and was indeed world renowned. There's an apocryphal story about a buyer from a prestigious New York dry goods firm who traveled to Calcutta with the intent of buying all the stock from a manufacturer there. When he arrived, he found that the buyer from Field & Leiter had already been there and beaten him to the goods. The New York buyer harangued the Indian manufacturer, claiming that Chicago was a desolate outpost and had no business making such an impressive purchase. The Calcutta merchant replied, "We know nothing about that, sir, but they discount their bills promptly."

They were also instrumental in driving the styles and tastes of the era, both due to the sheer size of their purchases and their careful advertising. Field believed that educating the customer would be in the best interest of both parties. This was especially helpful to the wholesale customers, who could trust the Field's salesman to supply them with the best quality and most desired goods that would sell quickly and turn a fair profit. It also carried over to the retail side, with ladies of the day learning to trust Field & Leiter to supply only the finest and most fashionable dry goods available. Even in the earliest days of the firm, owning an item from Field's carried a certain cache, an indication that the purchaser was of a sophisticated and discerning nature.

Oddly enough, retail sales actually composed only a small percentage of Field & Leiter's vast empire. In fact, Leiter would have been quite pleased to dispose of it altogether, but it was always Field's first love. Field also realized that the highly successful wholesale division allowed them to compete in retail in a manner that most couldn't. Instead of buying retail merchandise from a jobber at inflated prices, Field & Leiter simply skimmed some of the finest and newest products from their wholesale inventory, displayed it beautifully and were able to sell it for a lower price than the competition. It was inevitable that Field would soon long for grander quarters than their Lake Street location, and who better to help with that dream than Field's old friend, Potter Palmer?

During the few years since he'd been gone from the dry goods business, Palmer had not much heeded his doctor's admonition to slow down. Instead, he'd been buying up real estate at a fast pace. He had a vision of a new retail district, convenient to the railroad depots and farther removed from the foul-smelling Chicago River. The perfect location, he believed, was along State

Street. In most people's eyes, State Street was an unlikely spot to build new businesses, and many of his contemporaries openly mocked his grand plan. Although it was a main north–south thoroughfare, it was a slum district, lined with cheap boardinghouses, butcher shops, saloons and assorted shanties. The narrow street was muddy and rutted, and the only streetcar line was a "bobtail" car, pulled by horses along a single rail. It frequently jumped the track in the mud, leaving passengers to wade through the muck to their destination. While property on Lake Street, the "street of merchants," was selling for up to $2,000 a linear foot for frontage, State Street land could be had for a song. The most expensive, at the corner of State and Madison, ran about $500 a front foot in 1867, but farther south on State some properties sold for as little as $60 per front foot.

Palmer was not swayed by his critics, however, and was convinced that Lake Street was doomed to fail. Wedged in between the railroads and the sewage-filled river, it had no room to grow. The new railroad and streetcar lines all converged at State Street, making it a convenient place to reach from any area of the metropolis. It only needed someone with vision to make it happen, and Potter Palmer was nothing less than a visionary. He bought every lot he could until he held title to most of the frontage property on State Street between Lake Street and Quincy Avenue to the south, a distance of three-quarters of a mile. His first move was to tear down or set back each building he owned and persuade his remaining neighbors to do the same, so that the once-narrow street was now over one hundred feet wide. Instead of a cramped and grimy country lane, State Street now had aspirations to become a magnificent boulevard.

Next, Palmer tore down all the shacks on the southwest end of his properties and began construction on a majestic hotel at the corner of State and Quincy as a wedding gift to his new bride, Bertha Honore. The Palmer opened its doors to the public on September 26, 1871, only to burn to the ground thirteen days later in the great Chicago fire. Palmer, undeterred, immediately started construction on a new and even grander building, this time built of brick and iron, and later advertised as "The World's Only Fireproof Hotel."

While his first hotel was still being built to the south, Palmer began construction on a huge new retail palace on the north end of his holdings, at the corner of State and Washington Streets. The limestone and marble building towered six stories above the street, and the façade featured dramatic white Corinthian columns reaching toward the sky. By this point,

FIELD, LEITER & CO.'S BUILDING, STATE STREET.

Engraving of Field, Leiter & Company store before the Great Chicago Fire.

Palmer had spent well over $2 million funding his dream of a new business district. All he needed were the proper tenants, and he knew exactly where to look for them.

When he approached Field and Leiter about the grand store he was building, they were more than willing to listen. Palmer had never steered them wrong, and besides, the store on Lake Street was uncomfortably cramped and confining. Worse yet, in spite of their best efforts to maintain high standards, Lake Street itself was growing more crowded and dirty by the day. Although Palmer was asking a veritable fortune for rent—$50,000 per year—the chance to escape the ailing business district and forge new ground held an undeniable appeal. After short deliberation, the firm of Field & Leiter agreed to lead the pack and move to "Palmer's Palace."

The State Street grand opening was scheduled for Monday, October 12, 1868, but the Lake Street store remained open until the last possible moment. In the weeks leading up to the move, employees worked frantically at the close of each business day to transport merchandise between the two locations. Stock boys slept in the new store to stand guard over the inventory, while Chicago newspapers whipped the public into a shopping frenzy, promising the largest and finest retail establishment in the entire country. The store was stocked and ready by Saturday evening, but the partners agreed that no business should transpire on Sundays, the Lord's Day. On Lake Street, they had gone so far as to cover the display windows on Sundays, and the new location would be no different. Business would have to wait until Monday.

That Monday dawned bright and clear, and the partners, both junior and senior, stood ready to greet the throngs already gathered outside the doors. As they entered, each lady received a single red rose, and the gentlemen received an expensive cigar. Modern steam elevators carried visitors to the upper floors, which housed an incomprehensible array of wholesale goods. The uppermost floor was dedicated to packing and preparing wholesale orders, which then rode down in freight elevators to be whisked to destinations across the country. The enormity of the enterprise astounded most observers.

The real attraction, however, was the awe-inspiring first-floor retail emporium. The counters were a smooth dark walnut, which stood dramatically against white frescoed walls. New gas lighting fixtures cast a pleasant glow across the room, nothing like the dreary and dark establishments of the past. Merchandise of every description, sure to please every lady and gent, sprawled in attractive display against the counters, which were staffed by helpful and pleasant clerks. And, as always, Field's "satisfaction guarantee" promise went with every sale. The crowds were so thick that it was nearly impossible to move within the store. The newspapers gleefully reported on the smashing success, taking the opportunity to declare victory over lesser cities, some going so far as to suggest that Chicago retail had trumped even the East Coast's reigning monarch, the city of New York. From a *Chicago Tribune* editorial the morning following the grand opening:

> *The formal opening by Field, Leiter and Company of Potter Palmer's new marble palace on the corner of Washington and State was the grandest affair of its kind which ever transpired even in Chicago, the city of grand affairs... The attendance of wealth, beauty, and fashion which assembled*

last evening to take the benefit of the grand opening was something unparalleled in Chicago's history...[even] New York cannot boast such a gorgeous palace for the display of dry goods.

In sharp contrast to the newspapers' jubilance, Field's competitors watched glumly as they resolutely reviewed their own options. Some ran huge sales, placed bold advertisements and decorated their storefronts as an inducement to draw in customers, but the writing was on the wall: the bold move from Lake Street to State Street by the premier dry goods firm of Field & Leiter sounded the death knell for the old business district on Lake Street. Like it or not, the competitors knew they had to follow if they were to survive. Soon, a mass exodus occurred as one firm after another relocated along State Street. Once again, Palmer's foresight paid off handsomely for him and his associates, and the new retail boulevard thrives to this very day.

Chapter 3

FIRE AND SURVIVAL

Aftermath of the Great Chicago Fire

[I suffered] *no loss except by the fire of 1871. It swept away everything…*
There were no buildings of brick or stone left standing…the disaster was so
sweeping that some of the companies which had insured our property were blotted
out, and a long time passed before our claims against others were settled. We
managed, however, to start again.

October 1871 was a brutally dry month, the tail end of a drought that
had persisted since July. Strong southwest winds swirled leaves, dust
and other debris through the parched streets during the unseasonably warm
Indian summer. Dried leaves and twigs crackled underfoot, and tiny fires
seemed to spurt up everywhere. On Saturday, October 7, the members
of the Chicago Fire Department had spent much of the day successfully
fighting a large fire. Although they won the battle, it left them drained and
exhausted. The fledgling city did not yet have enough men or equipment to
keep up with the rapid population growth, and what they had was already
stretched to the limit by that October day. To make matters worse, many of
the buildings were constructed of wood, and crowded conditions made fires
more likely to spread. However, no one could predict the horror that was
brewing for the following day.

Sunday, October 8 dawned hazy and warm. It was a typical day for
most residents, who attended their chosen house of worship and spent

the afternoon tending to chores. Patrick and Catherine O'Leary, Irish immigrants who lived at 137 De Koven Street on the southwest side of the city, were no different. After a busy day, the family was preparing for bed about 9:00 p.m. when a neighbor pounded on their door to alert them to a fire in the alley behind their barn. A *Chicago Republican* writer, Michael Ahern, later wrote an admittedly false but enduring tale that attributed the fire to Catherine O'Leary's cow, which Ahern said kicked over a kerosene lantern and started the conflagration.

In reality, the cause of the blaze was never officially determined, but many suspect it was started accidentally by an O'Leary neighbor named Daniel "Peg Leg" Sullivan, so known because of his wooden leg. Sullivan's mother kept a cow in O'Leary's barn, and it's possible that Daniel started the fire while bringing feed to the animals, most likely through careless use of smoking materials. He did rescue the cows and alert the O'Leary family to the danger, but in later interviews investigators found numerous inconsistencies in his recounting of events, which appeared to them to be an attempt to remove himself from blame. In any event, the fire quickly spread, the burning embers driven northeast by the strong southwest wind. Ironically, the O'Leary house was spared as the fire raged onward toward the central business district.

One neighborhood resident ran to a nearby pharmacy and pulled the fire alarm while the fire was still quite small, but the guard at the station confused the location and sent the brigade in the wrong direction. By the time they realized their mistake, the flames were out of control. Originally, officials hoped that the fire would stop when it reached the south branch of the Chicago River, but wooden vessels moored along the shore provided fuel, and the strong winds whipped the embers across the river with ease.

When word of the advancing firestorm reached John Devlin, the head of Field & Leiter's stock department and a loyal and trusted employee, he was relaxing with friends on Fourteenth Street. Devlin watched as panicked crowds approached, fleeing ahead of the glowing orange sky. His stomach churned as he thought of the marble palace filled to the brim with expensive inventory. Jumping to his feet, he began to run with the crowd, clambering frantically over the Van Buren Street bridge just ahead of the flames. When he reached the store, Henry Willing and a few others were already there, trying to devise a plan. Other employees, loyal to a fault, arrived ready to help. Soon Leiter and Higinbotham joined them, and shortly thereafter Field arrived as well. At first, it looked as though the fire might swing to the west and bypass the store, but they couldn't be sure. The partners decided to move as much inventory as possible to Leiter's home on Calumet Avenue near Twenty-third Street, safely out of the path of the flames.

Higinbotham ran to the company's barns, rousing all the drivers and their horses. Private carriage firms were already working the business district, demanding large amounts of cash and dumping loads in the street if a better offer came along. Field & Leiter had its own loyal fleet and didn't have to contend with the piracy. Indeed, all the employees came together as a team in an effort to save their employer's business. One salesman ran to the basement to stoke the boilers and get the steam elevators operating in order to move merchandise quickly. Others formed a relay team of sorts, grabbing the most expensive and critical inventory and moving it to the company wagons waiting outside. Once the wagons were full, they would gallop off into the night to Leiter's home to deposit their valuable cargo and then quickly race the flames to return for another load. When they realized the trip to Leiter's home was taking too much precious time, the wagons simply dropped merchandise in a safe spot along the lakefront, leaving a burly stock boy or boiler tender to stand guard. Meanwhile, Devlin and several others headed for the roof, where three huge water tanks stood. Using hoses powered by basement pumps, they soaked the sides of the building, hoping to buy some time. Field and others soaked heavy blankets and draped them across windows.

As the night wore on, the city collapsed in shambles. Looters took to the streets, smashing windows and stealing or destroying whatever the fire had missed. Throngs of panicked and sometimes drunken people surged through the business district, wailing and seeking safety. People were trampled and clawed as others fought to escape the hellish heat. As the fire threatened the city's gasworks, attendants were forced to shut it down, and the fancy gaslights at the marble palace flickered out for the last time. Field and his employees resolutely continued to work by candlelight or by the glowing light from approaching flames.

By the early hours of Monday morning, the fire had reached the waterworks to the north and shut off the water supply. With no means left to fight the flames, the end was imminent. Soon the buildings on the east side of State Street just north of Field & Leiter were on fire, and a brief shift in the wind brought the flaming embers to "Palmer's palace." Moments after Devlin and the last of the employees evacuated the now burning building, their eyebrows singed and faces blackened with soot, it burst into spectacular

Remains of Field, Leiter & Company after the Chicago fire of 1871. Sign directs employees where to collect any pay due them.

flames. By 3:00 a.m., the store was completely ablaze, and over $2 million worth of inventory had been lost.

The night, however, was not over for the Field's crew. They needed to return to where they had dropped merchandise so that it could be moved to safer locations, away from looters and thieves. What wouldn't fit in Leiter's house was placed in a nearby schoolyard, covered with tarps and guarded around the clock. The partners gathered up all the blankets, bedding and inexpensive coats they had saved and donated them to the Chicago Relief and Aid Society, to be distributed to those in need.

The fire continued to burn until Tuesday morning, when diminishing winds and a light rainfall helped it burn itself out. The conflagration killed approximately three hundred people and burned four square miles of the city in a path of destruction that stretched for thirty-four city blocks. Damage estimates exceeded $220 million, one-third of the city's entire valuation. About ninety thousand people, nearly one-third of the population, were left homeless. Many believed that the city could not possibly recover from such a deadly blow, but Chicago had nothing if not spirit. The embers had barely cooled before residents and business owners began to clean up and rebuild.

Field and Leiter were no exception. All that remained of the once grand store were a few twisted beams and a pile of rubble, but within days, the partners posted a sign on the site, telling workers where they could come to collect any pay due them. Even in the midst of such terrible devastation, the employees' welfare was of paramount importance to the firm. Field knew what it was like to be poor and had a great deal of empathy for the struggling workers, many of whom lost everything they owned in the fire. The partners and higher-level employees, meanwhile, were gathered at Leiter's house to form a plan.

They quickly divided the urgent duties. Leiter would inventory all the rescued merchandise, while Field took on the task of finding a new location to reopen. Henry Willing immediately began to intercept all incoming freight and diverted it to a temporary warehouse in Valparaiso, Indiana. Harlow Higinbotham gathered up the hastily rescued ledgers of the firm and created a temporary office at his mother's home in Joliet, Illinois, about forty miles southwest of Chicago. He brought along the bookkeepers and accounting department, and they began the arduous task of determining the store's losses. For weeks, Higinbotham and his staff availed themselves of his mother's hospitality while they pored over ledgers and carefully compared records with the inventory counts being received from Leiter. The final tally was grim: about $2.5 million of inventory had gone up in flames. The firm had various insurance policies that, in theory, would cover about $2.2 million, but with almost the entire business district burned to the ground, everyone feared that insurance companies couldn't handle the overwhelming losses and would simply fold in the wake of the disaster. The loyal and tenacious Higinbotham wasn't about to sit idly and wait to see what happened. Instead, with his meticulous ledgers in hand, he hopped on the train and began to travel from city to city, visiting each of the insurers and politely requesting that their claim be settled immediately.

His strategy was a success. After two and a half months on the road, he returned to Chicago with about $1.3 million in insurance settlements in hand and another half million or so on the way. The final loss to the firm was approximately $750,000 in underinsured merchandise and unpaid claims. It was a great blow, no doubt, but it was considerably less in proportion to what most other merchants suffered.

In the meantime, Field was struggling to find new quarters, no easy task in a city that was essentially wiped out. He finally settled on a two-story brick horse car barn that was still standing at State and Twentieth Streets, owned by the Chicago City Railway Company. Moving from a great marble palace to a run-down horse stable was quite a dramatic change, but desperate circumstances required bold thinking. Field and workmen immediately set to work clearing out hay and gear, varnishing the floor and whitewashing walls. He knew that the first merchant to reopen would be swamped with business by people who needed to replace the basic necessities of life that had been lost in the fire. This appealed to Field as both a businessman and a humanitarian. He had the inventory, stacked at Leiter's house and queuing up at warehouses in Indiana; he just needed a place to bring it to the people.

On October 28, less than three weeks after the night of the fire, Field and Leiter reopened their wholesale division, and a week later, on November 6, the retail store opened for business. In this incredibly short span of time, they had turned a lowly stable into another fine emporium. Competitors were staggered, and once again Chicago newspapers gushed enthusiastically about the firm that seemed unstoppable. While other merchants held meetings to discuss ways to negotiate debt settlements, the partners quietly informed their creditors that they would be paying all debts in full and within terms. Their reputation, impeccable before the fire, was strengthened even more.

Of course, the new location was much too small to contain both retail and wholesale on a long-term basis. Just ten days after the fire, Field signed a contract for $140,000 to build a new brick structure at Madison and Market Streets to house the wholesale division. This unlikely west side location was in a poor district, but it was still accessible, unlike most of the central business district, which was buried in rubble and debris. Also, land here was dirt cheap, selling for as little as $5 to $7 per foot. Moving back to State Street wasn't an option at that point, at least until the land was cleared and readied for reconstruction, so the west side would have to do.

On March 4, 1872, the new five-story wholesale building opened with typical fanfare. The removal of wholesale inventory allowed the store on Twentieth Street to expand the retail selection and display area. For the first time in the firm's history, the two divisions were operating out of different locations. Due to changes in insurance underwriting after the great fire, the separation was a permanent one; it would have been impossible to obtain sufficient insurance coverage if both divisions were housed together. Other merchants, including Farwell & Company, followed Field to the west side, which quickly became the wholesale heart of the city. Once again, Field was a pied piper of sorts for fellow businessmen, who followed his lead

MARSHALL FIELD & CO.
WHOLESALE, CHICAGO

New wholesale building constructed after the Great Chicago Fire. The new building was necessary to keep wholesale and retail separate due to insurance company claim limits after 1871.

unquestioningly. The old horse barn turned a tidy profit but made only a small percentage compared to the formerly grand store on State. Leiter again brought up the subject of quitting retail, and once more Field refused to entertain the notion. In fact, within months, Field had commandeered a portion of the new wholesale building to open a small area known as "retail No. 2."

It soon became clear, however, that the poor industrialized west and south sides would never make a desirable location for a proper retail emporium, and Field began to watch for opportunities. His old friend Potter Palmer had talked about rebuilding the marble palace but soon changed his mind and sold the property to the Singer Manufacturing Company of sewing machine fame. Singer built a beautiful five-story limestone building on the site, approximately one-third larger than Palmer's old building. It featured a center atrium topped with a glass dome that flooded the floors with natural light. The building was quite attractive, with a light and airy feeling absent from most construction of the day. On October 9, 1873, two years to the day after the Chicago fire wiped out the central business district, Singer's new tenants opened for business: none other than the dry goods emporium of Field, Leiter & Company.

Although the partners might have breathed a sigh of relief, thinking their struggles were behind them, there was more disaster to follow. In September 1873, financier Jay Cooke and Company, long respected as one of the strongest financial institutions in the United States, suddenly closed its doors after being squeezed by inflation and speculation. Almost immediately banks began to fail, and five in Chicago shut down. Stocks dropped precipitously, and the value of merchandise tumbled. As other merchants panicked and refused credit, Field and Leiter did as they had in the last panic and stoically held the course. Once again, they continued to carry some of their better customers and freely offered any advice or assistance possible. They even went as far as sending managers to their clients' businesses, offering support and guidance.

This depression wasn't like the crash of 1865, which was relatively short-lived. This one lingered for several years and drove prices to rock bottom levels. In many instances, the partners were forced to sell merchandise at a loss in order to remain competitive. If Farwell lowered a price, Field lowered his even more. The firm's solid cash reserves helped, but much of what carried them was simple faith that the economy would eventually recover. When a reporter from the *Chicago Times* tried to goad Field into a hand-wringing session over dropping prices, he didn't succeed as he had hoped. "Will [dropping prices] suit you?" he asked Field. "Oh yes," replied the merchant prince, with a teasing grin. "We like to sell cheap. It pleases our customers."

Eventually, the economy did slowly recover. Chicago hadn't been impacted as badly as other major cities, although homelessness and unemployment were unacceptably high. Through it all, Field and Leiter kept their heads, remained true to their guiding principles and ended up coming through the lean years even healthier fiscally than they had begun. If they experienced a mild sense of déjà vu during the financial crash, however, what happened on November 14, 1877, must have sent chills down their spines.

On that date, a passerby noticed flames coming from the roof of the Singer Building on State Street. He rushed to pull a fire alarm, but as had happened in 1871, the responding brigade went to the wrong location, a building a few doors down the street. Word of the fire spread to local boardinghouses where dozens of Field's employees lived, and once again, the faithful rushed to the store. This time, however, the flames spread too quickly, and only a small fraction of the inventory was saved. Crowds of spectators blocked the street and hampered the salvage attempt. Although the building itself withstood the blaze, it was completely gutted and everything inside destroyed. Once again, the firm's retail division was temporarily homeless.

This time, Field wished to do better than a horse barn. He quickly set his sights on the exhibition building—formally known as the Inter-State Industrial Palace—that sat right on the lakefront. Although the building was spacious and attractive for its intended purpose, it was an unlikely spot for a retail store. The lakefront location was beautiful during temperate weather, but during winter it became a hellish frozen place with howling winds and bone-numbing cold. But the rent was beyond cheap at only $750 per month, and it was immediately available. Two days after the fire, Field announced the new temporary location would be ready in time for Christmas shoppers. And so, on November 27, the store opened, despite a heavy rainstorm that continued for three days. It was stocked partly with salvaged merchandise from the State Street store, selling for heavily discounted prices, and new fancy merchandise taken from the wholesale division.

Even the drenching rain and wind couldn't discourage the loyal shoppers. Lines snaked around the building, and the store filled so quickly with customers that guards and policemen had to keep the doors shut, only allowing a new group in as earlier customers departed and freed up some room. Even though the opening was a tremendous success, Field knew the location's limitations made it unfeasible for a permanent store. To mitigate some of the accessibility issues, he arranged an expensive omnibus service

Engraving of the Exhibition Building where Field & Leiter relocated after the second devastating fire in 1877.

Portrait of
Marshall Field in
his forties, during
his partnership
with Leiter.

to pick up shoppers at the corner of State and Randolph every five minutes
and deposit them directly at the exhibition hall's front door.

While Field searched for a more permanent location, the Singer Company
wasted no time in rebuilding at the corner of State and Washington. Once
again, a new marble palace began to rise from the ashes at that corner.
In the spring of 1878, Field and Leiter moved retail once again, this time
to another temporary location on Wabash Avenue. Field knew in his heart
that they belonged at State and Washington, but by this time Leiter was
completely fed up with retail and wanted to close the division. The tension
between the partners grew, but Leiter was always subordinate to Field and
resisted a serious confrontation. He glumly agreed to return to the State

Street location, and the partners agreed to buy the building this time instead of renting.

During the reconstruction, the Singer Company had always assumed that Field and Leiter would return to the rebuilt store, and they were more than happy to consider an outright sale. At the time, Field was on a buying trip to New York, so Leiter agreed to attend to the negotiations. Unfortunately, the somewhat stubborn and irascible Leiter immediately angered Singer officials when they named what he considered to be an unreasonable price. The asking price was $700,000. Leiter fumed that he would pay not a penny more than $500,000 and said, "If we don't take the building, you won't find another tenant in Chicago for it!" Leiter was wrong—they could and they did, promptly leasing the space to rival retailer Carson, Pirie and Company for $700,000 per year.

Field was furious at Leiter's mishandling of the situation and raced back from New York to salvage the deal. With no bargaining power left, he was forced to agree to the full asking price of $700,000. Even worse, he was now the proud owner of a beautiful building that was leased to his competition! Carson and Pirie were well aware of the awkward position into which this placed Field, and they weren't about to make it easy on him. The clever Scots agreed to forfeit their lease, but it would cost Field another $100,000 cash. Reluctantly, he paid, and Field and Leiter were once again back at State and Washington, this time for good. After eight years of bad luck, it seemed that the tide was finally turning. Unfortunately, the chasm between the two partners was wider than ever.

Chapter 4

CHANGE AND PHILANTHROPY

The Merchant's Final Years

It is only in the wider public affairs, where money is a moving force toward the general welfare, that the possessor of it can possibly find pleasure, and that only doing constantly more.

Marshall Field was undoubtedly a man who lived by his principles. He believed in hard work, honesty and service to his fellow man, and he cultivated and rewarded these traits in others. By 1880, the firm of Field & Leiter boasted a total of seven partners. In reality, only two—Field and Leiter—had invested any significant capital, and Field was by far the majority partner. The others, including Lorenzo Woodhouse, Henry Willing, Harlow Higinbotham and brothers Joseph and Henry Field, had each been awarded a small partnership interest in reward for their excellent service and commitment to the firm. Field and the five junior partners held a shared vision for the future that included a fabulous retail division. Leiter was the odd man out.

Leiter's distaste for retail and his extreme caution annoyed Field, but more troubling were his quick temper and increasingly hostile attitude. He once threw a potential wholesale customer out of the building—loudly proclaiming him a sneak and a thief—only because the man's jet black mustache coupled with gray hair led Leiter to conclude he had dyed the offending facial hair in an apparent act of moral turpitude. On another occasion, he flew into a rage when a young salesman, John G. Shedd, brought him an $800 sales ticket from a customer with a poor credit record. The flustered and embarrassed customer explained that he intended to pay in cash for his purchases, but Leiter would have none of it. "We don't want your business! Get out!" he shouted.

By 1881, Field had run out of patience. The partnership agreement between the principals was expiring, and Field informed Leiter that he had no desire to renew it. He told Leiter that he was willing to either buy him out or entertain an offer to be bought out himself. Leiter knew it was the end. He had always worked the financial end of the business and didn't have the skills, vision or perhaps even desire to run the company without Field. He had never taken an active hands-on approach to the operational side

Marshall Field & Co.

CHICAGO, Market and Madison Sts.
NEW YORK, 104 Worth Street.
MANCHESTER, 37 Faulkner Street.
PARIS, 46 Rue des Petites Ecuries

Chicago, Jan. 26, 1881.

The Copartnership heretofore existing under the firm name and style of Field, Leiter & Co. is this day dissolved by mutual agreement of the members thereof. Mr. L. Z. Leiter retiring from said firm.

MARSHALL FIELD.
LEVI Z. LEITER.
LORENZO G. WOODHOUSE.
HENRY J. WILLING.
HARLOW N. HIGINBOTHAM.
JOSEPH N. FIELD.
HENRY FIELD.

The business of the late firm of Field, Leiter & Co., in all its departments, will be continued by the undersigned, under the name and style of MARSHALL FIELD & CO.

MARSHALL FIELD.
LORENZO G. WOODHOUSE.
HENRY J. WILLING.
HARLOW N. HIGINBOTHAM.
JOSEPH N. FIELD.
HENRY FIELD.

Very respectfully,

MARSHALL FIELD & CO.

Announcement of Leiter's retirement and name change to "Marshall Field & Company."

of the business and didn't relate well with the other partners. In January 1881, Leiter quietly announced his "retirement" from the firm. Effective immediately, the firm's name would be Marshall Field & Company.

Of course, Leiter didn't require any sympathy. By this time he was a very wealthy man with major real estate holdings, and his sudden and unplanned retirement allowed him to travel with his socialite wife and enjoy a life of leisure. When reporters pressed him for his future plans, Leiter replied, "I'm going trout fishing!"

Field, for his part, could now freely implement his plans without an overly cautious and sometimes hostile partner to slow him down. In his usual style, however, he trusted his associates to do what they were best at and kept his interference to a minimum. Although he had his hands into seemingly every aspect of the business, he didn't micromanage. He would ask pertinent questions, listen intently and then often say, "Use your best judgment."

It was this environment that brought out the best in his employees and cultivated intense loyalty to both the firm and the man. Hard work and good character paid off at Field's store, and the lowliest employee had the same opportunity to rise to the top as more experienced hires. When a twenty-two-year-old New England farm boy named John Graves Shedd applied for a position with Field and Leiter in 1872, Field offered him a position as a stock boy in linens for a salary of ten dollars per week. It was less than Shedd had made at his previous sales position in Vermont, but he sensed opportunity with Field. In much the same way that the young Field had worked diligently to prove his worth with Cooley & Farwell, Shedd vowed to make his mark on Field & Company. He didn't disappoint.

One of his earliest successes involved a revolutionary change in purchasing methods. Shedd noticed that at the end of each season, some sizes or colors remained unsold, whereas others sold through quite early. Buyers of the day simply bought according to manufacturer's recommendations or based on personal hunches, with little regard to customer preferences. Shedd believed there was a better way. With permission from his boss, Henry Willing, Shedd carefully reviewed past sales ledgers and devised a formula to determine the sell-through, or "turns," of each item. Now buyers could stock up, for example, on certain sizes and buy fewer of others. Field studied the proposal and believed it had merit. He instructed Willing to put the new system in place in the ladies' neckwear and lace department for a trial period. In that department, sales doubled within a year, and Shedd's system became the basis for all purchasing.

Shedd advanced rapidly in the firm, from sales to merchandising to management, and in 1892 he was awarded a small partnership. Shedd had settled into the position of running the company's entire wholesale division, and soon Field's was second only to H.B. Claflin of New York in wholesale volume. By 1886, the firm had outgrown the wholesale building on Market Street, and Field commissioned renowned Boston architect Henry Hobson Richardson to build a new and larger facility on property Field owned slightly to the south. In June 1887, the imposing seven-story granite and brownstone behemoth opened, filling an entire city block bounded by Adams, Quincy, Wells and Franklin. With more space came more product choices: hardware, musical instruments, furniture, clocks, baby buggies—in short, anything the late nineteenth-century shopper could ever imagine or desire.

Marshall Field's 1897 hardware catalogue. By this time, the store had expanded far beyond dry goods.

Hundreds of temporary workers had to be brought in to assist with inventory each year.

Dockworkers preparing to load wholesale orders into company wagons.

Once, an interviewer asked Field how he could afford to pay Shedd such a high salary. Field considered the question a moment and replied, "I can't afford *not* to." Indeed, the young Vermont man had grown into an indispensable member of the company and one that Field respected and relied upon. The same interviewer, sensing Field's message, then asked, "What would you do if he left your employ?" Field, with just a hint of a smile, said, "I'd hire another stock boy." This exchange truly illustrates the great man's predilection for cultivating talent from within his organization. He believed no work was too humble to be disregarded, and those with talent could climb the rungs to success. "Cream rises to the top," he often claimed.

Shedd wasn't the only employee who enjoyed a rapid rise to the top. Harry Gordon Selfridge, an energetic young man from Jackson, Michigan, started with the firm in 1879. Like Shedd, he began as a ten-dollar-a-week stock boy. Also like Shedd, he had grand aspirations for success. That is, however, where the similarities ended. Shedd was careful and studied; Selfridge was exuberant, dramatic and hurried. He soon gained the nickname "mile-a-minute Harry" for his breathless speech and rapid gait. He was quickly promoted to salesman in the wholesale division and did quite well, but Field thought he'd be an asset for retail. Selfridge accepted and hit the division like a hurricane.

Unlike Shedd, who had enjoyed a great deal of support and encouragement from his manager, Henry Willing, Selfridge immediately locked horns with the retail superintendent, J.M. Fleming. Fleming considered the young man brash and vulgar. Selfridge considered Fleming a rusty old dinosaur who was preventing retail from growth. Selfridge, however, was not about to back down. When Fleming sniffed in disdain at one of his many ideas, he would simply march to Field's office and plead his case. Field might have agreed with Fleming about the young man's brash nature, but Field could see beyond that and saw a man with vision and an unerring instinct for what the customer wanted. Invariably, Mr. Field would instruct Fleming to "give it a chance, and see if it makes us money." It almost always did. Soon, Selfridge was promoted to run the entire retail division, with Fleming reporting to him.

In 1889, flush with success and perhaps a little cocky, Selfridge walked into Field's office and requested a partnership interest. Field was stunned and more than a little angry at the young man's audacity. It wasn't that Selfridge didn't *deserve* the perk, but Field was taken aback that someone had overstepped his boundaries and actually *asked* for the honor. "You'll

Above: Trade cards, such as this one from Home Decorative Arts Department, were the precursors to today's business cards.

Right: By the early part of the twentieth century, motorized vans began to show up alongside horse-drawn wagons.

get your partnership, Mr. Selfridge!" rumbled Field. And so, in 1890, Selfridge was awarded a 2/85th share, with Field loaning him the $200,000 in required capital.

One of the things that made Selfridge so successful was his way with people, both customers and employees. He held many of the same cherished beliefs as Field, such as "the customer is always right" and "cream rises to the top." He excelled at motivating his staff and continued Field's way of cultivating loyalty and innovation. One employee, Homer Buckley, summed it up: "He'd inspire you; make you feel you knew how to do things; and he'd do it by talking it out with you, treating you with respect…never talk down to you…I never met a man capable of putting such inspiration into his employees."

Under Selfridge's capable hand, retail flourished. The firm began an expansion that marched down State Street to Randolph and east to Wabash. One by one, it acquired other buildings and added them to the complex. In 1890, show windows were added to the original store, which allowed Field's to gracefully showcase its beautiful goods to the passing pedestrians. The first annex opened in 1893 at the corner of Washington and Wabash, a nine-story building designed specifically for retail. And, in 1898, it expanded the State and Washington building upward: the original mansard roof was removed and two more floors were added, making that building eight stories high. Finally, in 1902, the ragtag group of buildings north of the original State and Washington store that had been hobbled together over the years was torn down, and construction began to create a uniform and attractive frontage.

Charles B. Atwood of D.H. Burnham and Company designed the new building, but he died before it was completed. The firm's namesake, Daniel Burnham, was a master architect who designed city plans for not just Chicago but also Cleveland, San Francisco and Baltimore and created the famed "White City" of the 1893 World's Columbian Exposition in Chicago. Nothing but the best would do for Field's, and the retail palace they created was at that time the largest in the world. The construction was finished in stages, with sections opened in 1902, 1906, 1907 and 1914. Marshall Field & Company's retail store now filled an entire city block, bounded by State, Randolph, Wabash and Washington. It included several beautiful atria, including a thirteen-story sky-lit dome in the northwest section and a five-story-high mosaic dome designed by Louis Comfort Tiffany in the southwest corner. There could be no question of retail supremacy in Chicago; Marshall

Freight tunnels under State Street allowed for delivery of goods, mail and coal and served as a utilities easement for telephone cables.

Field, long known internationally through its foreign buying offices for wholesale trade, now was the world leader in retail as well.

Selfridge, for his part, was beginning to chafe at remaining a small junior partner. In 1901, Field decided to change the ownership structure from a partnership into a corporation, thus ensuring a smooth continuation of operation upon his death. In February, 60,000 shares of stock with a par value of $100 were issued, for a total capitalization of $6 million. Marshall Field retained 34,000 shares; John Shedd, Robert Fair (a top wholesale executive) and Joseph Field split another 20,000, for 6,666 2/3 each; and Selfridge received 6,000 shares. Field served as president of the new corporation, and Shedd was named vice-president.

Selfridge had always had a somewhat contentious rivalry with Shedd, and this new development most likely added to his rancor. In 1904, he approached Field and told him that he was leaving to open his own store. Although surprised, Field said little other than to wish him success. Selfridge purchased the entire interest of Schlesinger and Mayer, a smaller State Street retailer, for a reported sum of $5 million. From the start, he regretted the move. The employees were not like those at Field's. They lacked the same work ethic and enthusiasm, and he quickly found himself overwhelmed and with no one qualified to offer support. "There are a million things to do and nobody to do them!" he complained. After just three months in the business, he wanted out.

He sheepishly turned to his old rival, John Shedd, for help. Shedd knew that Carson, Pirie, Scott & Company had previously wanted to buy out Schlesinger and Mayer, more to acquire its location in the beautiful Louis Sullivan–designed building at State and Madison than anything else. The firm had ached for a State Street location since 1879, when Field had paid them to surrender their lease on the Singer building, and the State and Madison property was one of the finest in the city after Field's imposing edifice. With Shedd acting as a broker, Selfridge was able to recoup his original investment, plus a $250,000 "bonus." Carson's continued to occupy

Washington Street and Wabash Avenue store annex in the early 1900s.

State Street store in the early 1900s.

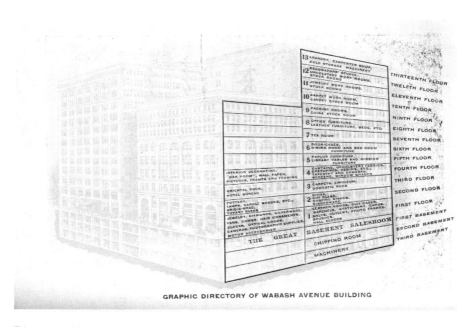

Directory of Wabash Avenue annex in the early 1900s.

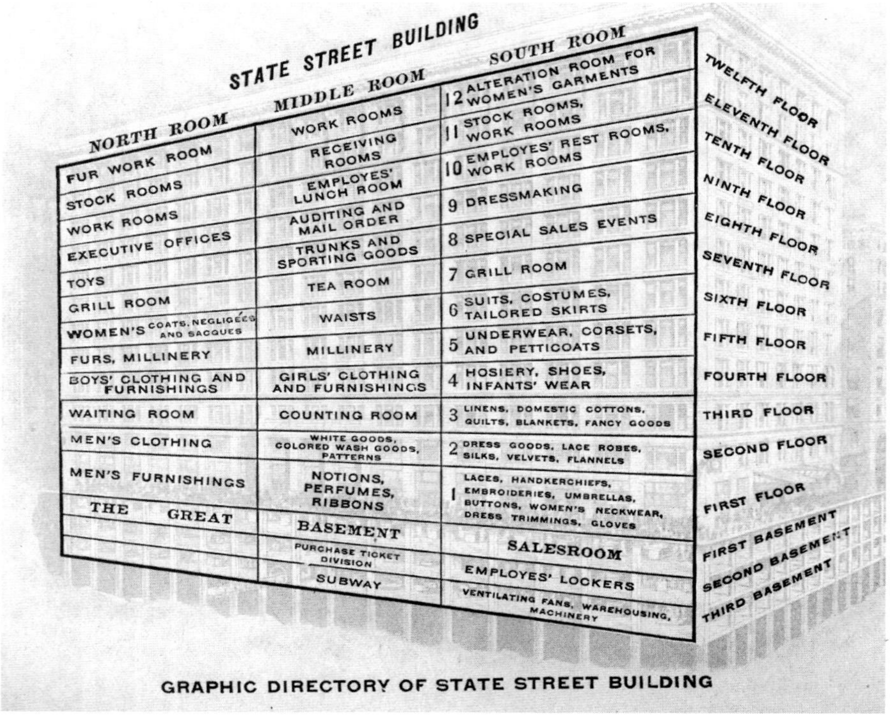

GRAPHIC DIRECTORY OF STATE STREET BUILDING

Directory of State Street store in the early 1900s.

the store for over one hundred years, finally moving out in 2007 so that the property could be redeveloped.

Selfridge, meanwhile, disappeared from view for a few years. In 1909, his old associates were surprised to hear an announcement that Harry Gordon Selfridge was opening a spectacular retail emporium on Oxford Street in London, England. Starting from scratch this time, "mile-a-minute Harry" created his new business after the Field model, incorporating the ideas and philosophies that had made the American merchant a legend in his time. The new store was a resounding success. Selfridge's is still one of England's premier retailers and now boasts four stores throughout the country. Until the day he died, Selfridge kept a portrait of his mentor, Marshall Field, in a prominent position above his desk.

As Field was approaching his later years, he remained intensely involved with the store, walking through it on a daily basis, asking questions and greeting employees. However, he allowed his trusted team to tend to the

Marshall Field's residence on Prairie Street was in a wealthy district that is now part of the National Register of Historic Places and a Chicago landmark.

daily operations. Although business was successful beyond Field's wildest dreams, his personal life had become quite lonely. In 1892, his wife Nannie departed to France with the children for an extended "vacation." She never returned and died there a few years later. Field lived in a large mansion on Prairie Avenue, with just the servants or occasional visitors for company. His daughter, Ethel, had married and remained in England. His son, Marshall Jr., had returned to Chicago but was a troubled young man without the obvious interest or ability to step into his father's shoes, and he caused the elder Field much worry. Only grandson Marshall Field III, the apple of the old man's eye, always brought a smile to his face when visiting.

One of the other bright spots in the aging man's life was his friendship with Arthur Caton, a wealthy lawyer and avid sportsman, and his wife, Delia. Field spent a great deal of time with the couple, enjoying their hospitality and companionship. In early 1905, Arthur Caton died. That summer, Field invited the young and lively Delia to accompany him on a trip to England. To the surprise of those back home, Marshall and Delia wed on September 5 in St. Margaret's Church in London. The marriage seemingly revitalized

Field, and the happy couple returned to Chicago and its lively social scene. They attended operas and horse shows, often with Marshall III in tow.

By now, Field's wealth was estimated at over $120 million, and his philanthropy was becoming more obvious. He had always been generous, if cautious, with his wealth. It was common for Field to loan money to new businessmen or join a worthy cause. Now, however, he was truly making a difference in the city he loved. He was a major sponsor of the 1893 World's Columbian Exposition and later (somewhat begrudgingly) gave $1 million to keep open the Columbian Museum in Jackson Park, one of the few permanent structures from the fair. It was renamed the Field Museum of Natural History in his honor, and he left an additional $8 million endowment to his namesake in his will. Field Museum remained in Jackson Park until 1921, when it was relocated to the museum campus along the lakefront near downtown, where it stands to this day.

Along with John Rockefeller, Field was also a prime benefactor of the University of Chicago, donating 10 acres of land and substantial cash to help get the fledgling school on its feet. The school's football field was known as Marshall Field for many years, until it was later renamed Stagg Field after coach Amos Alonzo Stagg, the first tenured football coach in America.

His philanthropy wasn't limited to Chicago, his adopted city; he also created a wonderful library in Conway, his birth town in Massachusetts. He served as a trustee at the First Presbyterian Church and donated generously to that and several other churches of various denominations. It's estimated that in just the last decade of the nineteenth century, Field gave over $3 million to various charities. Of course, that figure just includes notable donations and not the smaller gifts he handed out routinely to smaller causes.

Marshall Field donated land and funding to help build the University of Chicago, a favored charity of his friend John D. Rockefeller. *Courtesy of Wikimedia Commons.*

Field Museum of Natural History was founded in large part with contributions from Marshall Field and named in his honor. *Courtesy of Wikimedia Commons.*

Unfortunately, although he had finally found happiness with his beloved Delia, it was short-lived. On November 22, 1905, Field and Delia were in New York when he received notice that his son, Marshall II, had been shot and was in critical condition at Chicago's Mercy Hospital. The elder Field raced back to Chicago and maintained a vigil at his son's bedside, but there was little hope. Five days later, he succumbed to his injury.

The circumstances surrounding his death were unclear. The attending physician claimed that Marshall II had said it was an accident upon admission. The younger Field's servants claimed they had heard a shot and found the mortally wounded man lying on the floor with an automatic pistol nearby, leading many to speculate it was a suicide. He was known to be depressed and perhaps even unstable, so that theory was certainly plausible. Much evidence at the time, however, pointed to an even darker explanation: the young man was a frequent patron of the Everleigh Club, a high-class brothel on South Dearborn Street. The word on the street was that he was shot by one of the prostitutes after an altercation. With no solid evidence, and perhaps to spare his famous father the embarrassment, the coroner's jury ruled it an accidental self-inflicted shooting.

Field took his only son's death terribly hard and seemed to suddenly age, appearing old and frail. Shedd and others tried their best to keep him occupied and involved, but he was lethargic and somber. Only Delia could coax an occasional tentative smile out of him. On New Year's Day 1906, Field agreed to join his nephew Stanley Field and friends James Simpson and Robert Todd Lincoln in an impromptu game of golf in the snow. The trio used red balls and played a full eighteen holes despite the bitter cold. Later, Field spent some time discussing business with Stanley. "You're the one of the family I've got to rely on," he reminded his nephew.

Portrait of Marshall Field at age seventy-one, shortly before his death.

After his snowy golf escapade, Field mentioned he had a sore throat, which quickly developed into a miserable cold. Despite the illness, he and Delia boarded a New York–bound train in mid-January so that he could tend to some business related to his railroad holdings. When they arrived on January 15, Field was so weak that he could barely walk to the couple's suite at the Holland House. Delia notified Stanley, who rushed to New York along with Dr. Frank Billings, a highly respected Chicago physician. When they arrived, it was clear that Field was suffering from pneumonia, and his condition rapidly deteriorated despite Dr. Billing's best efforts. On January 16, with Stanley and Delia at his side, the world's greatest merchant died.

When word reached Chicago, business at the store was immediately suspended. Shades were drawn and employees sent home. Their collective grief was palpable. It seemed as though the very essence of the enterprise had been extinguished. A few days later, when his body was returned to Chicago for the funeral, it was like nothing the city had never seen. On a sleet-filled gray morning four days after his death, most of the business district shut down to honor the man who had contributed so much to its establishment. All the stores on State Street were dark, and the Chicago Board of Trade shut down at noon. Flags flew at half-mast throughout the city, and deep lavender mourning ribbons sprouted from every lapel. Even major wholesale houses in New York closed their doors for the day as a gesture of respect. As the funeral procession wound slowly through streets lined with untold thousands of mourners, the sleet fell harder, as if the sky itself was lamenting the great man's passing. He was laid to rest at Graceland Cemetery on the north side, near Nannie, his first wife, and Marshall II, the son who had preceded him in death by just two months.

Chapter 5

CONTINUING THE VISION

The John Shedd Years

The man whom I believe to be the greatest merchant in the United States…that man is John G. Shedd.

Although the city—indeed the world—mourned the loss of the man who had built an empire based on honesty, integrity and service to others, the store that bore his name forged ahead, more determined than ever to carry on the legacy.

Due to Field's careful foresight in planning his organization, the chain of command was clear. John Shedd would assume the presidency. Stanley Field, Marshall's beloved nephew, was named as vice-president. James Simpson, who had served for many years as Field's personal assistant and confidante, stepped up to the position of second vice-president. At this point, most of the original partners were gone. Higinbotham had retired in 1901 as a wealthy man. Lorenzo Woodhouse died in New York in 1903, a few years after retirement. Henry Willing and Henry Field had both retired in 1883, before the incorporation. Joseph Field continued his association with the firm but remained in Europe to supervise the foreign buying operations. In any case, there was no doubt that, with Shedd at the helm, the business would continue in the exact manner Field had intended. For the remainder of his long career at Marshall Field & Company, Shedd, like Selfridge, kept a large portrait of Field above his desk and each day filled

John G. Shedd ascended to presidency of Marshall Field & Company after the founder's death.

a vase with two red roses in remembrance of the beloved founder and his personal mentor.

Shedd continued the rebuilding and modernization of the State Street store as he and Field had envisioned. By late 1907, the section once occupied by the Singer Building had been completed, finally creating an unbroken expanse of granite, marble and display windows along the full block-long frontage on State. The new store was twelve stories high, built atop 252 solid concrete caissons driven 90 to 110 feet into the ground and resting on solid rock. Nearly twenty thousand tons of structural steel was used in construction. At one point, when steel was scarce and construction slowed, Shedd contacted the chairman of the United States Steel Corporation, Elbert Gary, an old friend of Field's. Gary promised to see to it personally that Field's marvelous new store had access to any and all steel needed to complete construction.

The granite monoliths that still flank the State Street entrance soar 48 feet, 9 inches into the sky and have a diameter of 3½ feet, qualifying them

State Street main entrance, flanked by marble columns that are among the tallest in the world.

Spacious main aisle of State Street store, early 1900s.

Above: State Street Fur Salon, 1907.

Left: The State Street Louis Comfort Tiffany dome is over six thousand square feet and is composed of 1.6 million individual pieces of Favrile art glass. *Photo by Peter Rimsa.*

as some of the largest in the world. Inside, the main aisle stretched for 385 feet, past smooth walnut and glass display cases. The store boasted over 1.5 million square feet—more than 35 acres—of selling floor, including a full basement used for "budget items," an idea that took hold and flourished during Selfridge's reign. Freight tunnels run under the store, and an underground pedestrian pedway was added to provide access to the new Store for Men on Wabash Street when it opened in 1914 across the street from the main store.

Inside the southwest corner of the store, a Tiffany mosaic dome unlike anything ever seen by Chicagoans or tourists alike still causes those who enter to gape in awe at the splendor overhead. It remains the largest mosaic of its kind and is made up of over 1.6 million pieces of iridescent Favrile glass, each set by hand by a crew of fifty artisans. It took a year and a half to complete the massive project. The reconstructed store also included spacious and comfortable restrooms for men and women, a true novelty in those days, as well as ladies' writing rooms equipped with stationery and a telephone exchange that was the busiest private exchange in the world, handling over ten thousand calls per day.

Employee facilities included a library, spacious restrooms and a fully staffed hospital room for emergencies. In accordance with Field's beliefs on

Marshall Field's switchboard was the busiest private exchange in the country.

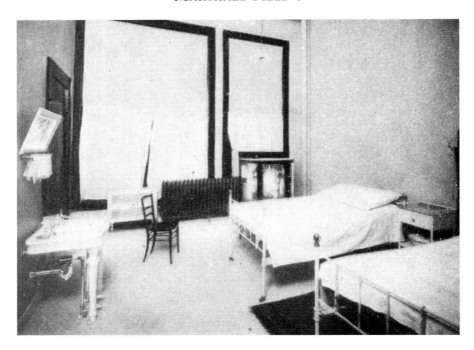

The State Street store was a city in a city, with even a medical facility staffed by nurses.

The pleasant and inviting reading room allowed guests to relax and meet with friends in the store.

self-education, employees were always encouraged to read and take training classes to improve themselves and, thus, their position in life. It was a benefit to the company as well, evidenced by the many who rose through the ranks to positions of authority.

The store also offered "information" and "accommodation" bureaus. The information bureau could provide arrival and departure times for trains, as well as ocean and lake steamers; explain railway routes and points of interest; and provide city maps or other items of information. The accommodation bureau allowed customers to send and receive telegrams and cables; provided local and long-distance telephone service; made sleeping car and cab arrangements; checked bags; wrapped and sent parcels; sold theater tickets; and offered customers the advantage of a stenographer's services. Of course, these were just the posted services. At one time, while Field was still alive, a gentleman mentioned to a clerk in the wholesale division that he was mourning the accidental estrangement of his brother, who had traveled to Europe and lost contact. The word went out to Field's foreign buying offices, and in a short amount of time the wayward sibling was located, and the brothers reunited. There was almost nothing that Field and his employees would not do to please a customer or offer a helping hand to someone in need.

The idea of in-store restaurants, which had begun with a humble tearoom in 1890, soon expanded, and by 1920 there were seven places a weary and hungry guest could dine: the Circassian paneled Walnut Room, the beautiful Narcissus Fountain Room, the North Grill Room, the Wabash Avenue Tea Room, the Colonial Quick Service Tea Room, the Wedgwood Room and the Men's Grill in the Store for Men.

The Walnut Room, which opened in 1907, is recognized as the first full-service restaurant in a department store. Originally named the South Tea Room and later the Walnut Grill, it is the only one of the original restaurants still in operation today. The room's namesake dark Russian Circassian walnut paneling, coupled with massive crystal chandeliers, white tablecloths and attentive staff, all combined to create an atmosphere of luxurious class and comfort. The Walnut Room becomes a special oasis at Christmastime, when a three-story-tall and splendidly decorated Christmas tree takes center stage in the room.

The Narcissus Room, which opened in 1914, was modeled after a fine Italian *ristorante*, complete with elegantly tiled floors and a Carrara marble fountain reproduced from one in Pompeii. A bronze statue of Narcissus,

Marshall Field's had the first foreign buying office and eventually expanded all over Europe and parts of Asia.

A child admires goldfish in the pond inside the luxurious Walnut Room restaurant. *Courtesy of Susan Greene.*

the Greek and Roman mythological figure known for beauty, sat atop the fountain, and the large windows gave guests a beautiful view of nearby Lake Michigan. The Narcissus restaurant was closed to the public in 1987 and now serves as a special event room.

The Men's Grill opened in 1914 in the new Store for Men, a twenty-one-story structure across the street on Washington. As mentioned earlier, an underground pedway connected it to the main building so that patrons didn't need to brave Chicago's challenging weather. Legend has it that the idea for the store was conceived after Shedd was once trapped on an elevator with a portly gentleman smoking a large cigar. As he puffed away, the ladies on the elevator coughed and covered their faces with handkerchiefs. Shedd strode to his office and said to his counterparts "Let's get men out of this building!"

Whether the story is true or not, the move did make perfect sense. By offering a separate shopping haven for men, the store could focus on the preferences and needs of each gender. Ladies could spend the day surrounded by fine silks and household items; men could examine a vast array of sporting goods and gentlemanly attire. The tearooms on State

The Sportsman's Department in the Men's Store sold sporting goods and apparel of every imaginable kind.

Street were mostly light, airy places filled with ferns and wicker and offering dainty meals; the Men's Grill was dark and clublike, with lots of mahogany and burnished leather chairs. The menu leaned toward steak, and good cigars were always welcome.

Although retail sales were growing at an amazing pace, Shedd was not forgetting the wholesale division from whence he came. Wholesale sales still made up the bulk of the firm's profits, but competition was tough. He knew that the only way to compete was by offering absolutely the best merchandise at fair prices. If customers understood that the quality and support they received from Field & Company was far superior to any other wholesaler, Shedd could steer them away from shopping strictly by price.

In order to do that, Shedd began looking at the manufacturing process itself. Field's had long been buying the entire output of factories, but those factories used the same materials and manufacturing processes of those that supplied the competitors. Shedd knew that, in order to stand out from the crowd, he would need to somehow raise the quality at the manufacturing level.

To begin, buyers began to present the factories with strict guidelines for quality. For example, typical China-made rugs of the day had 100 fibers, or "strings" per foot. Field's buyers insisted on a minimum of 120 fibers per foot, creating a denser, softer and longer-lasting product. They also provided designs to the makers that were richer in color and more complex than standard, resulting in a premium carpet unmatched by competition.

This attention to detail carried into even small handmade products. At the time, nearly all hairbrushes were made in Japan by home-based artisans. Field's buyers drew up a list of specifications and sourced better materials for the workers. These guidelines were then translated into Japanese and dispersed throughout the region by the firm's buying office in Kobe. The end result was of such high quality that the Japanese government created a bureau for inspection of brushmaking, using Field's guidelines as the standard. In short order, the Field's name was synonymous with quality throughout the world.

In the quest for quality, Shedd poured a great deal of money into several southern factories, most notably Spray, Draper and Leaksville, North Carolina. The trio of towns were within a few miles of one another, situated near water power and large coal deposits. The Spray mill produced woolen blankets; two mills in Draper produced cotton and wool blankets and sheeting; and the Leaksville plant produced satin and crocheted bedspreads and knitted underwear. Despite the investment, the mills' owner experienced financial and quality problems. Eventually, Field's stepped in and bought the plants outright, as well as a mill in Fieldale, Virginia, that produced Turkish towels and fine damask napkins and tablecloths. They immediately upgraded the equipment to the newest state-of-the-art and looked for other ways to improve.

Now that Shedd owned mills that dominated several small towns, it occurred to him that the factories would be more productive and quality-conscious if the residents were happy, healthy and educated. Thus began Field's experimentation into "company towns." The concept wasn't unusual—many coal mines and other industries effectively operated towns in the region—but under Shedd's hand, it would be carried out with the same devotion to quality that led the firm.

Field's began to build schools, homes and other facilities. The small but neat houses featured all the latest conveniences, including electric lighting and clean water. These were then leased to employees at a very modest rent. Single employees could live in company-built boardinghouses and enjoy meals prepared by a registered dietician. Medical care and vocational training were made available to all. Visiting nurses traveled from home to home giving free instructions on disease prevention and care of the sick. Although Field's insisted its moves weren't paternalistic, it was true that the townsfolk were completely dependent upon the company for employment, shelter and education. Naturally, Shedd's idea paid off; production and quality skyrocketed in the mills.

Later, Shedd added numerous other factories to the Field's portfolio, including a lace factory in Zion, Illinois; a muslin manufacturer in New York; a silk plant in Union Hill, New Jersey; a fine rug company in Philadelphia; and dozens of smaller manufacturers scattered throughout Chicago. In addition, the State Street store itself had numerous workshops. The jewelry

Zion Lace Industries in Zion, Illinois, was one of the many textile and manufacturing plants purchased by Field's to supply quality products to customers.

Marshall Field's supplied almost everything a customer could want, from cameras to eyeglasses. *Photo by Peter Rimsa.*

workroom produced everything from fine jewelry to silver tea services to optical lenses and frames. It had its own foundry and worked with precious metals and stones of any description. An in-store boot and shoe plant did leather repairs and created fine custom footwear, including orthopedic models prescribed by physicians. A cold storage section for furs consisted of three vaults, which typically housed upward of $12 million in precious furs during any given season.

One of the most enduring departments was the Field's Candy Kitchen, which operated from 1929 until 1999, when demand overwhelmed the facility and then-owner Dayton-Hudson closed it and outsourced the production to Gertrude Hawk Chocolates in Dunmore, Pennsylvania. The Candy Kitchen produced chocolate and pastries of every style and description, bride's boxes, birthday collections in colors to match each month's birthstone and convalescent baskets. The hands-down most popular, however, were the legendary Frango mints, which exist to this day.

The origin of the name "Frango" is somewhat of a mystery. The original Frango was created in 1918 as a frozen dessert by Seattle-based Frederick & Nelson department store. The popular story persists that the desserts were originally named "Franco" after **FR**ederick **A**nd **N**elson **CO**mpany but later changed to "Frango" due to the unwanted association with Generalísimo Franco of Spain and his brutal regime. It's a nice story, but the timeline doesn't work; the Frango name was trademarked in 1918, but Franco didn't

Left: Field's huge candy department sold handmade confections to an appreciative public.

Below: The bustling candy kitchen on the thirteenth floor of the State Street store manufactured Frango mints and other confections for over seventy years, until it finally closed in 1999.

A replica of an original Frederick & Nelson Frango container, early 1900s. *Photo by Peter Rimsa.*

Frederick & Nelson was the historic Seattle department store founded in 1890 and later purchased by Marshall Field's.

come into power until 1936. There are several other theories, but none that can be verified.

At any rate, in 1927, Ray Alden, who ran Frederick & Nelson's candy kitchen, designed a meltaway mint under the Frango name that was an instant hit. It consisted of chocolate from both African and South American cocoa beans, triple-distilled Oregan peppermint oil and local butter. In 1929, Marshall Field's acquired both the store and its trademarked Frango brand. Ever since, the Pacific Northwest creation has gained a Chicago identity.

Under Shedd's direction and exacting adherence to Field's priciples, Marshall Field & Company was now the largest retailer in the city of Chicago and the largest wholesale and dry goods company in the world. Now it was time to follow in his beloved founder's footsteps in philanthopy as well.

He was a founding member of the Commercial Club of Chicago, a civic group that worked to mold Chicago into a world-class city. The group promoted Daniel Burnham's 1909 Plan of Chicago, which recommended paved and widened streets and new parks, railroads and harbor facilities. They also championed reform issues such as street cleaning and sanitation,

The window display department was unrivaled in creativity and execution.

The Shedd Aquarium was a gift to Chicago from John G. Shedd, Field's president after the founder's death.

old-age pensions and programs to prevent juvenile delinquency. The 1909 Burnham plan is to this day regarded as one of the most influential urban planning documents ever created.

In the early 1920s, Shedd donated $3 million to construct a spectacular inland aquarium, then the largest in the world. Construction began in 1927, and the marvel opened to the public in May 1930. Unfortunately, Shedd died in 1926 after the plans were completed and never lived to see his namesake exhibit through to fruition. His widow, Mary R. Shedd, cut the ribbon at the opening ceremony.

The Shedd Aquarium is located on Chicago's lakefront museum campus, next to the Field Museum of Natural History. In order to bring the seawater and fish inland, a special railroad car named "the Nautilus" was built. It took twenty railcars eight round trips between Chicago and Key West, Florida to fill the Shedd's tanks, with a total capacity at the time of 1 million gallons. The aquarium is still one of the top attractions in Chicago and has been expanded several times to include exhibits such as a 3-million-gallon oceanarium that houses marine mammals including Beluga whales and Pacific dolphins and a 400,000-gallon shark exhibit.

Chapter 6

PROGRESS AND DESPAIR

The Great Depression and the World's Fair

National progress is the sum of individual industry, energy, and uprightness.

After Shedd's retirement in 1922, James Simpson, Field's former personal assistant, stepped up to the position of president. By that time, retail was growing at a phenomenal pace, and Simpson was ready to expand.

The first new Field's retail store opened May 1928 in Market Square in Lake Forest, Illinois, an uppercrust suburb on Chicago's north shore. It was followed later that year by another branch in downtown Evanston, also on the north side, and in 1929 by a French Renaissance–style building in Oak Park, a growing western suburb. All three suburbs were wealthy and possessed thriving business districts, in keeping with Field's reputation of catering to an upscale and increasingly urban clientele.

Also in 1929, the Marshall Field Garden Apartments were built by Field's grandson, Marshall III. The complex is a large non-governmental subsidized housing project, built to provide affordable housing for poor residents. The ten buildings cover two city blocks and contain 628 units. Unlike other low-income housing of the era, it offered educational and cultural opportunities for the residents and included open courtyards and play areas to foster a community-like atmosphere. At the time of its construction, it was the largest housing project of its type in the United States, and it still stands today.

Below: The Oak Park Store

Below: Market Square, Lake Forest

By the late 1920s, Field's had begun suburban expansion, with stores in Evanston, Oak Park and Lake Forest, Illinois.

In spite of the optimism, few could predict that the country was soon to be plunged into massive economic disaster. The wholesale division was turning a healthy profit, despite some lingering concerns about its future direction. The trend of manufacturers selling direct to business clients and bypassing the wholesale distributors created some disturbing ripples in the industry, but Simpson and his associates believed that the business could be revitalized. In 1927, the firm announced plans to build a massive trade center on land along the Chicago River.

The river, which had once caused so much consternation among residents due to its pollution and sewage, had undergone major changes since the early days of the Lake Street business district. In the 1890s, a new group, the Chicago Sanitary District, was formed to cope with the sanitation demands of the city. In 1900, the district installed a series of locks at the river's mouth that caused it to flow backward into the newly built Sanitary and Ship Canal, in one of the most remarkable engineering feats of the century. The change in direction kept the lakefront water supply clean, and fresh water from the lake helped flush pollution from the river. Although hardly changed into a pristine stream, the river no longer

Marshall Field Garden Apartments was privately subsidized low-income housing, designed to foster a sense of community among residents.

The community children's room at Marshall Field Garden Apartments.

A resident and child at their apartment in Marshall Field Gardens.

created an intolerable stench. In fact, by the end of the twentieth century, the Chicago River was clean enough to support sport fishing.

The proposed site for Simpson's new building was the north bank, just east of Wolf Point, the location of Chicago's first trading post. The area housed the original Wells' Street railroad depot, which closed in 1911 when a new and larger passenger terminal was built nearby. The abandoned railroad yard was an eyesore, and civic leaders were only too happy to support redevelopment. The finished building, known as the Merchandise Mart (or simply "the Mart"), was the world's largest building at the time, with over 4 million square feet of floor space. It held that distinction until 1943, when the Pentagon was built with floor space of 6.5 million square feet. In fact, for several of its pre–World War II years, the building housed many government offices that were later moved to the Pentagon.

The Art Deco–style marble, brick and concrete building was designed to be a "city within a city" and served to bring together vendors and trade from across the country. Marshall Field & Company consolidated all its warehouses

The Merchandise Mart, once the world's largest building, was built by Marshall Field & Company to house its wholesale division.

A row of delivery vans at the Polk Street warehouse, which was designed for Marshall Field's by architect Daniel Burnham.

and occupied the first four floors when the Mart opened in 1930, several months into the Great Depression, but soon cut back to one and a half floors as the Depression continued to take its toll on the company. Although Field's business returned as the economy improved later in the decade, the

Above: Telephone order department at Marshall Field's, about 1950.

Left: Evening view of the Merchandise Mart. It was sold to the Kennedy family in 1945.

wholesale division would never return to its previous robustness. Throughout the early 1930s, it continued to drag down the company's profits, and the once-thriving division was liquidated in 1936. The Merchandise Mart was later sold to the Kennedy family and remains an important part of Chicago trade to this day.

Simpson retired in 1930, but not before bringing several successful changes to the retail division. As mentioned in the last chapter, Field's bought out Seattle's Frederick and Nelson Company in 1929, at that time a $12 million a year business. D.E. Frederick, son of a wealthy Georgia plantation owner, and his partner Nels Nelson, a recently arrived Swedish immigrant, had founded the store in 1890. In 1907, Nels died at sea, and Frederick carried on alone. He was a great admirer of Marshall Field and in 1918 established a premier retail operation on Pine Street in Seattle, closely modeled after Field's store. It was an instant success and soon developed a reputation as the West Coast's finest.

When Frederick decided to retire in 1929, he wanted to sell his store but had rather definite ideas about who should be the successor to his empire. He declared that he "would only sell to Marshall Field and Company" and traveled to Chicago to speak with Simpson. He arrived without an appointment, and Simpson was not in, so he scribbled his intentions to sell on the flap of an envelope. When Simson received the rather primitive offer, he was delighted, and the deal finally came together in July 1929.

In 1930, as the Depression loomed and sales fell off, one of Simpson's last acts was to release some of the company's stocks to the general public as a way to raise much-needed capital. Of the 2 million shares authorized, 540,000 were offered at an opening price of fifty dollars per share, 200,000 were reserved for sale to employees and the balance were retained by existing stockholders. Simpson retired and left for a tiger-hunting trip to India, although he maintained a position as chairman of the board until 1932. In his wake, new corporate president John McKinlay assumed the complicated and precarious business.

McKinlay had been with the firm since 1888, when he joined as a $2.25 a week "cash boy." Now he found himself facing perhaps the biggest challenge in the company's history, the Great Depression. In spite of the economy, retail was still doing rather well, but, as mentioned earlier, wholesale losses created a drag on cash flow. He begged Harry Shedd, John's nephew, for help. Harry had long been working in Field's wholesale division and was an experienced manager. Shedd immediately began to eliminate outdated

Marshall Field's stock certificate. The store's shares first went public in 1930.

and money-losing lines, but he soon realized there was nowhere to stop; wholesale itself was largely outdated and bleeding cash.

In desperation, Shedd contacted Marshall III, Field's grandson and a member of the board. After some discussion, Field decided to bring in expert outside help. His choice was James O. McKinsey, a University of Chicago professor and founder of the McKinsey and Company consulting firm. McKinsey spent months reviewing the company's business, and his opinion was that wholesale must go. McKinlay and Shedd were both reluctant to institute the sweeping and drastic changes demanded, so the board placed McKinsey in the position of chairman, which had been vacated by Simpson in 1932. Now McKinlay and Shedd had to answer to him. Shedd, still unable to completely destroy the division his uncle had so loved, pleaded for a gradual wind-down of the business. McKinsey refused, and Shedd resigned.

Within a year, McKinlay left as well. McKinsey brought in some of his own people from the outside and quickly finished the job he had set out to do. By 1936, Marshall Field & Company was no longer in the wholesale business, with the exception of a few house brands such as Fieldcrest. McKinsey, despite his perhaps sincere intentions, was viewed as an "outsider" and battled

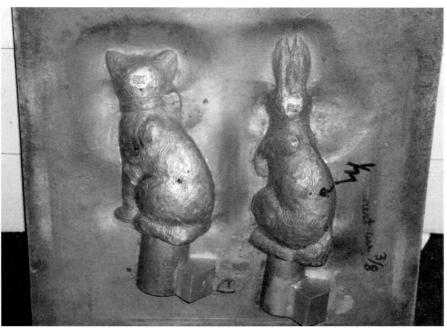

This page: Foundry mold for cat and rabbit doorstops manufactured exclusively for Marshall Field & Company. *Courtesy Michael Russell, Great Estate, Oshkosh, Wisconsin.*

continuously with management and stockholders until his death in late 1937. In his wake, two longtime Field's employees stepped into power: Hughston McBain, a longtime assistant to ex-president McKinlay, rose to vice-president, and Frederick D. Corley ascended from vice-president to president.

As troubling as the 1930s were for the company in general, and wholesale in particular, the decade did have its bright spots. In 1933, the Century of Progress Exhibition opened in Chicago. This world's fair celebrating Chicago's centennial stretched for miles along the lakefront and drew crowds from across the globe. It was originally intended to run until November 1933, but it was such a phenomenal success that promoters reopened it

Chicago's lakefront, aerial view, 1940s.

the following year as well. During its two-year run, it attracted nearly fifty million visitors.

The theme of the exhibition was technology and innovation. In fact, the fair's dramatic 1933 opening ceremony demonstrated technology in a novel way: when light from the rays of the star Arcturus were detected on the opening evening, it was focused on photoelectric cells in a series of astronomical observatories and then transmitted to Chicago in the form of electrical energy. This energy turned on the electric lights and signified the start of the fair. Arcturus was chosen because it had last appeared brightly in the sky during the World's Columbian Exposition in Chicago in 1893.

State Street store escalators designed by Westinghouse Company, 1932.

Early Westinghouse radio station. Marshall Field's was one of the first merchants to advertise by radio in Chicago.

Of course, Marshall Field & Company couldn't pass up the opportunity to embrace technology either. McKinlay, before the disastrous showdown of wholesale that resulted in his resignation, had spent much time spiffing up the store, replacing fixtures and installing new lighting. His biggest and boldest move, however, was the installation of electric escalators in the State Street store. Although escalators had been around for a while—Harrod's of London installed one in 1898—most were clumsy and noisy devices, certainly not in keeping with Field's quiet elegance. But McKinlay was convinced that a properly designed model would be a hit with the public and contacted Westinghouse Company to design one.

After rejecting several designs, the company finally hit upon the modern aluminum-faced model with safe rubber treads. The revolutionary and quiet new machines were installed at a cost of $600,000, just in time to impress the fairgoers. Field's had once again secured its place as a modern and sophisticated retail palace.

Chapter 7

FROM THE CITY
TO THE SUBURBS

The Changing Face of Retail

Those who enter to buy, support me. Those who come to flatter, please me. Those who complain, teach me how I may please others so that more will come. Only those hurt me who are displeased but do not complain.

With the Great Depression behind them and the wholesale division gone, Field's entered into a new period of stability. World War II had brought forth an era of increased public spending and prosperity, but it had also brought its share of problems for the company. There was, of course, a great shortage of goods, especially the Parisian fashions so loved by Field's clientele. Many of the company's best workers had gone off to war, some never to return.

The store sold war bonds and featured blood drives to support the war effort and used ingenuity to work around shortages. When metal was unavailable to manufacture hinges, in-house craftsmen designed wooden hinges. The company's remaining factories produced large quantities of war goods, such as parachute cloth, camouflage netting, wool blankets and uniforms, keeping a healthy balance sheet despite the uncertainty. In 1945, as the war was ending, Field's sold the Merchandise Mart to the Kennedy family, freeing up more much-needed capital. It was time, the company knew, to reevaluate.

Since McBain and Corley had assumed the reins, they realized that the shopping habits of modern consumers had changed. Women were tending

Above: By the 1950s, Chicago had grown into a business center filled with skyscrapers.

Left: Marshall Field III takes over his grandfather's fortune on his fiftieth birthday.

The Marshall Field's Choral Society boasted over two hundred members when it began in 1906. *Photo by Peter Rimsa.*

to shop more at small specialty dress shops, especially since the war shortages. People were beginning a migration to the suburbs, fueled by the postwar boom in housing. To some, the city itself seemed slightly out of date. Tastes were changing, and modern women expected and demanded more than they had in the past—more conveniences, more opportunities—and unless the store was willing to grow and change along with consumer tastes, it risked being relegated to the status of a dowdy old aunt.

To reestablish itself as a fashion center, Field's opened the ultra-exclusive 28 Shop in 1941. The salon was named for the department's private elevator entrance at 28 East Washington and also for its twenty-eight dressing rooms, individually decorated in groups of two. One pair had ceilings lined with fine lace; another set was fitted up with exotic bamboo. It was a popular destination for debutante gowns and the latest designer fashions. Women shopping in the 28 Shop were treated like royalty, in a store already known for exquisite customer service. A lady could nibble on lunch while the highly trained staff brought her

The After Five
Room offered
evening gowns
and formal
apparel.

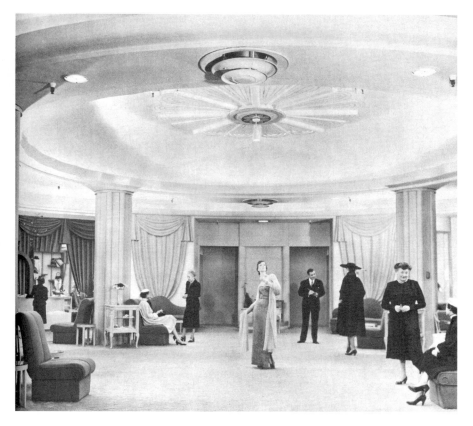

The 28 Shop, an exclusive designer boutique, acquired its name from its private entrance at 28 East Washington.

everything she wished to try on, from delicate lingerie to luxurious fur coats and handmade shoes.

In its heyday, stately limos would pull up to the private entrance to disgorge their privileged passengers, who would then be whisked directly to the salon without having to pass through the crowds of mere mortals in the main store. The 28 Shop served as the site of many private benefits and charity fashion shows after the rest of the store closed for the evening.

Field's also brought high fashion to the masses with impromptu fashion shows in the seventh-floor tearooms. Beautiful models in couture clothes, decked out in the latest accessories, strolled through the restaurants several times a week, allowing the luncheon crowd to see the newest offerings from French and British designers. Everything from resort wear to evening gowns

Check your car with uniformed attendants at Randolph St. entrance, near Wabash Ave.

Your car will be delivered at Randolph St. entrance within 10 minutes after you call. Ask any floorman.

A MODERN PARKING SERVICE

At New Reduced Rates

A service which eliminates all worries of automobile parking is available to customers of Marshall Field & Company at moderate cost. No longer need the problem of finding a parking space prevent you from driving to the downtown district in your car. Simply follow these directions:

1. Drive to Randolph Street entrance of Marshall Field & Company, near Wabash Avenue.

2. Check your car with uniformed attendant. He will drive it to Central Chicago Garages, Inc., a few blocks north, where it will be parked in safety.

3. Present your check to uniformed attendant, or inform any floorman in the store when you are ready for car. It will be delivered to you within 10 minutes after you call, at Randolph Street entrance near Wabash Avenue.

A general garage service is available while car is parked. Washing. Polishing. Simonizing. Vacuum cleaning of Upholstery. Service repairing. Tires and tire repairing. Battery service and inspection, and other services. If service is desired, give instructions upon checking car.

Field's parking service took the concept of valet parking to another level, offering automobile services along with valet service.

PARKING RATES

This service includes all transfer charges from Marshall Field & Company to the Central Chicago Garages, Inc., and return.

Up to 2 Hours 50c
Up to 4 Hours 60c
4 to 12 Hours 75c

If desired, car will be delivered at any theatre, club or other point away from the Marshall Field & Company store. For this service, there is a small additional charge.

Information regarding rates for general garage service, including repairs, washing, polishing and other services, will be supplied by uniformed attendants, Randolph Street entrance, near Wabash Avenue.

MARSHALL FIELD
& COMPANY

Offers an Improved

PARKING SERVICE

For the Convenience of Customers

Operated by
CENTRAL CHICAGO GARAGES, Inc.

Field's parking service rates were quite a bargain.

was displayed. For those customers who didn't have the means to afford such frivolities, the Field's staff would gladly help them translate the latest looks into a less-expensive, but still high-quality, ensemble.

Another new specialty at that time was the beautiful Bride's Room. The store had been the first to introduce a bridal registry back in 1924 and had long sold wedding gowns and other apparel, but this new offering gathered everything needed for wedding planning into one department. Advertising at the time painted a picture of romanticism at its best:

> *The sentimental swish of a gleaming satin gown and the nostalgic rustle of bridesmaids' dresses mark the romantic science of wedding planning... here...you can translate your dreams into the once-in-a-lifetime reality of a wedding gown and veil...Here you can gather advice on photographs and flowers, on effective color schemes and appropriate attire for everyone in your party.*

The Bride's Room offered all types of wedding services and planning.

Field's was one of the first to offer charge plates to its customers. *Photo by Peter Rimsa.*

The Millinery Department sold hats of every price and description. *Photo by Peter Rimsa.*

Trained wedding counselors stood at attention, ready to assist the blushing bride-to-be with any facet of her special day.

It wasn't necessary to get married, however, to receive special assistance. Field pioneered the concept of personal shoppers, and the Tip to Toe Shop created a staging area for their efforts. They could help a shopper coordinate an entire season's wardrobe or simply put together a polished look for a special occasion. Their job was to assemble clothing and accessories from throughout the vast store, and the customer didn't even have to show up in person to get the job done.

Once, the wife of a politician in a far-away state wrote to Field's that her husband was likely to be elected to public office, and she was at a loss to choose the appropriate style of dress. The personal shopper pulled together a complete wardrobe and sent it to her via air express. The customer was thrilled and, along with her thanks, extended an invitation to the Field's shopper to attend the inaugural ball.

New clothing styles weren't the only fashions Field's showcased. Management put a stronger emphasis on home goods and interior decorating with the addition of the Trend House in 1938. This five-room house on the eighth floor showcased the latest in furniture styles and designs and was completely redecorated a few times a year. Visitors could walk through and see the colors, accessories and furnishings combined into a pleasing display. The in-store Home Planner's Bureau was also available to help if viewing the Trend House wasn't inspiration enough.

Other departments were added or spruced up, including the book department. Originally added in 1914, it was a popular spot that developed the practice of authors' book signings. It featured the Collector's Corner, filled with rare first editions and old leather-bound volumes. In the 1950s, the Field's book department was touted as "the largest in the hemisphere." One famous event that took place there in 1944, however, generated a little more excitement than Field's had anticipated.

Bennet Botsford was a publishing executive with Rand McNally and a great animal lover. When his company published the children's book *The Elegant Elephant* by Russell McCracken, he decided it would be a great marketing gimmick to bring a live elephant named Judy into the third-floor book department to "autograph" copies with a rubber stamp attached to her trunk. Judy rode up in the freight elevator and generated massive crowds all day long. She was patient and obedient—right up until it was time to leave. She stubbornly refused to set foot onto the freight elevator, no matter

Fine silverware from Field's graced many houses. *Courtesy of Susan Greene.*

how much her handlers wheedled and threatened. It was a battle of wills, and the elephant won. To dislodge the reluctant pachyderm from the store, workmen had to build ramps down three flights of stairs, and only then could the trainers lead her down to the street.

Despite all the wonderful changes at the flagship store, Field's leaders knew that they still needed to expand beyond State Street if they were to survive the twentieth century. The answer was clear. They would follow the customers to the suburbs and build grand new shopping districts if necessary. The three original suburban stores were small facilities in established town shopping areas. The Oak Park store, for example, carried only women's and some children's clothing, yet it still managed a respectable business.

In 1951, Field's revenues had grown to a record $225 million a year. In order to generate additional cash for an ambitious suburban expansion, the company divested itself of all remaining manufacturing operations in 1953.

Above: The Music Department sold everything from instruments to record players. *Courtesy of Susan Greene.*

Right: Cash registers in each department eventually took the place of cash boys. *Courtesy of Susan Greene.*

The Music Department carried a vast array of popular music albums. *Courtesy of Susan Greene.*

Fieldcrest Mills was sold to Amoskeag Company and later evolved into the powerful Fieldcrest Cannon Company.

After 1953, the company raced to the suburbs at astonishing speed. A south suburban Park Forest location had opened earlier that decade in Park Forest Plaza, a new shopping area owned by developer Philip Klutznick. In 1956, Field's teamed up with Klutznick to create a huge new open-air shopping center in north suburban Skokie, on land already owned by Field's. The center would be anchored by a large new Marshall Field's store.

There's an apocryphal story about how the center got its name: it was said that executives struggled in frustration to name the new development, discarding one name after another. One evening at a business dinner, chairman McBain mentioned the difficulty to Mrs. Stanley Field, wife of Marshall's nephew. She promptly suggested the name "Old Orchard." McBain loved the idea and surmised that Mrs. Field must be quite an expert

Right: Rajah, a green-winged macaw, was a longtime resident of the Toy Department. *Courtesy of Susan Greene.*

Below: The mural in the Music Department on State Street. *Courtesy of Susan Greene.*

on Chicago history, because Orchard Place was the original name for the big Chicago airport recently renamed O'Hare Field. "Oh no," laughed Mrs. Field. She explained that when Stanley Field first came courting, her father couldn't remember the name "Field" and mistakenly referred to him as "Mr. Orchard." The nickname stuck within the family, and Stanley's in-laws still referred to him as "Old Orchard." Although it's a cute anecdote, it is much more likely the name did come from the nearby airport, which still carries the three-letter Federal Aviation Authority airport code of ORD to this day.

Other stores quickly followed: Mayfair Mall in suburban Milwaukee, Wisconsin, in 1959; Oakbrook Center in Oak Brook, Illinois, in 1962; River Oaks Center in Calumet City, Illinois, in 1966; and Woodfield Mall in Schaumburg, Illinois, in 1971. Woodfield was, for many years, the nation's largest shopping center, and it still is the largest mall in suburban Chicago. Its name was derived from its two major tenants: Sears' board chairman Robert E. Wood and, of course, Marshall Field.

Between 1973 and 1982, ten more stores were added: eight in Illinois and two in Texas. The Chicago stores included Rockford and Vernon Hills in 1973; Water Tower Place in Chicago and Aurora, both in 1975; Orland Park in 1976; Joliet in 1978; West Dundee in 1980; and Bloomingdale in

The popular Hawthorn Room Restaurant at Marshall Field's Old Orchard store in Skokie, Illinois.

Marshall Field & Company				PAY PERIOD ENDING	
				S 003964 100701	05-25-68
				DEDUCTIONS	
DESCRIPTION	HOURS	EARNINGS	MEMO	DESCRIPTION	AMOUNT
REGULAR	11.00	18.15		WITHHOLDING	2.03
				SOC.SECURITY	.80

		YEAR TO DATE					
HOURS	EARNINGS	WITH. TAX	SOC. SEC. TAX	STATE TAX	CITY TAX		
266 75	547 58	50 66	24 08			NET PAY	15.32
22-01-08 FORM 9		* DENOTES CREDIT				SEE REVERSE SIDE	

In the 1960s, part-time workers often spent more than they earned. *Courtesy of Susan Greene.*

1981. In Texas, the Houston Galleria store opened in 1979, and Dallas followed in 1982.

During these years, Field's didn't just open new stores, it also acquired several small department store chains across the country: the Crescent in Washington state in 1962; Halle Brothers in Ohio, 1970; J.B. Ivey in North Carolina and Florida, 1980; Union Company in Ohio, 1980; Lipman's in Oregon, 1980; and several Liberty House stores in Washington state, also in 1980.

In keeping with the tradition of in-store restaurants begun at State Street, most of these stores featured restaurants or tearooms, and food service became a large part of the company's focus. Field's even stepped outside of the retail arena and tried its hand at freestanding restaurants when, in 1948, it opened in two locations at Chicago's bustling Midway Airport. On the first floor of the new passenger terminal on Cicero Avenue, Field's opened a coffee shop known as the Blue and Gold Cafe. It was designed to provide quick and casual snacks to weary travelers, but famous guests such as Frank Sinatra frequented it as well. With its long, steel lunch counter and checkerboard tile floor, it looked as if it had been taken right out of an Edward Hopper painting.

For the fine dining that Field's guests had come to expect, the Cloud Room Restaurant on the second floor provided a place to meet and enjoy a leisurely meal, all while watching the planes taxi past. A Calder mobile hung from the ceiling, and famous guests included Marilyn Monroe, Jimmy

The Cloud Room at Midway Airport in Chicago offered fine dining to weary travelers.

Stewart and Clark Gable. In 1951, a complete dinner featuring roast leg of veal, gravy, new parsley potatoes and Danish red cabbage sold for $1.80. Field's maintained a staff of 180 to keep the restaurants running twenty-four hours a day so that incoming passengers could be greeted by the famous Field's name before they even left the airport. It was an exciting new age, and Field's intended to move with the times.

Unfortunately, by the early 1960s, most of the airlines were moving to the new airport west of the city, O'Hare International, and Midway became a ghost town, nearly abandoned except for a handful of corporate planes and small private aircraft. The Cloud Room and the Blue and Gold Cafe both closed in 1962, victims of the progress they had tried to emulate. Ironically, in the latter part of the century, congestion at O'Hare became so intense that the City of Chicago was forced to revitalize Midway to relieve some of the pressure, and these days Midway is busier than it ever was. Sadly, chain restaurants and sandwich shops stand where the elegant Cloud Room once beckoned guests to relax, soak up the ambiance and enjoy a fine meal.

Chapter 8

A CHILD'S DREAM

Christmas at Field's

Uncle Mistletoe, says he, wants the boys and girls to be
In his Kindness Club to stay, if they're kind and good each day
Not just one day, not just two, but, be kind the whole year through
Oh...
Do a kind deed, say a kind thing, smile a big smile, everyone sing
—from "The Kindness Club Song," 1949

Christmas in Chicago was a special time. Electric lights twinkled, and snow glistened on the ground, just right for an impromptu snowball fight. The bitter cold wind off the lakefront nipped at ears and faces, turning cheeks rosy. Frozen breaths hung in the air, suspended like cartoon balloons over the heads of passersby. All these signs pointed to just one thing: it was time to visit Marshall Field's!

Although Marshall Field's State Street store held allure all year round, the anticipation that built up as the holidays approached was legendary to generations of Chicagoans. From its earliest days, the store produced beautiful window displays to draw in shoppers, but the Christmas windows continued to expand, until by the mid-1940s they took over the entire store.

The fourth-floor Toy Department carried dolls of every description.

The grand Christmas tradition had its roots during the Depression, when in 1934 the State Street Council came up with the idea of a holiday parade to stimulate sales during the difficult economy. It became a yearly event, and competition grew fierce between the merchants to see who could create the most festive decorations. Never to be outdone, Field's put its best talent to the task, and each year improved upon the past. The planning would begin in February, when the display managers gathered to choose a theme. The concept was sketched out, discussed, tweaked and sketched again. Finally, when everyone was in agreement, the work began in earnest.

Toy buyers would immediately head out to factories, both at home and abroad, to purchase the best selection of the newest and most enticing toys to fill Santa's sleigh. Display teams began the arduous task of creating all the fixtures, decorations and props needed to bring the vision to life. Many of the figures were animated and, in the early days, had mechanisms that required winding every hour. Later, of course, electricity handled the job. By early July, winter merchandise and decorations depicting snowy scenes began to queue up in earnest, in stark contrast to the beastly hot and humid weather of the Chicago summer outside.

your little girl can learn while she plays with this

Mirro aluminum cook and bake set

$2

16 pieces, each one just like yours, packed in a big, bright box. There is a whistling tea kettle that really works, double boiler with cover, pie plates, cookie sheet, fluted mold, mixing bowl, muffin pan, bird mold, scoop, measuring cup and four cookie cutters. When you make cookies, she can make hers right along with you! Knobs are red enamel; and to give you an idea of size, the double boiler is 3½ in. high. For girls 3 to 10 years old.

151W4 cook and bake set, $2
estimated postage, 14c

waffle iron, toaster, mixer, lemonade set—all in this

little deb appliance set

$4 95

Three of the most popular appliances are included in this set. They're non-electric, but all have cords with suction cups that attach to the wall just like real. The hand-operated mixer really works and has a movable arm, speed indicator and mixing bowl. The waffle iron has plastic base and trim plus a tray and plastic bowl and pitcher. The metal toaster has a pop-up lever just like yours, and the lemonade set consists of pitcher and four glasses in metal holder. You'll find your own appliances are left alone when your little daughter has these for her very own. Mixer is 7½ in. high. For children 3 to 10 years.

151W5 appliance set, $4.95
estimated postage, 22c

Toys—Fourth Floor, Middle, Wabash. Also Evanston, Oak Park and Lake Forest   15

A 1950s ad showed baking toys for little girls.

It was also time to begin hiring and training the seasonal personnel who would be required to reinforce the ranks during the busiest shopping days of the year. State Street typically added about four thousand part-time employees each season, all of whom were as carefully trained as the full-time staff. Field's developed training films that coached the newcomers on proper deportment and the store's history, as well as the more mundane tasks of cashiering and wrapping goods. In one such film, the Roman god Jupiter, patron deity of social order, gently strums a harp while emphasizing the importance of courtesy and respect. During the busiest days of the season, when employees were stretched to their limits, the store would

a thrill for every boy on your Christmas list!

16-piece mechanical freight train set

$4.95 accessories extra

Nothing will thrill a boy more than a train of his very own. This mechanical freight train set makes a pretty impressive sight when it's all set up. For $4.95 you get a streamlined locomotive with automatic bell, tender, box car with sliding doors, sand car and caboose. Also included are six pieces of curved track, four straight tracks and a crossover. The engine and cars are made of heavy-gauge steel, lithographed in bright, true-to-life colors. The key that winds the powerful spring is set in the engine so it can't be removed and lost.

Add to the realism of the set by ordering the accessories shown above. The tunnel is lithographed with bright mountain scenery. The metal water tower has a spout that can be manually raised or lowered. The train bridge is finished in satin aluminum—looks just like the real thing. All these accessories may be ordered separately, and all will fit any mechanical or electric train.

154W2   mechanical train set, $4.95, estimated postage, 18c
154W3   train tunnel, $1.50, estimated postage, 12c
154W4   water tower, $1.75, estimated postage, 10c
154W5   train bridge, $1, estimated postage, 10c

Mechanical Toys—Fourth Floor, Middle, Wabash. Also Evanston, Oak Park and Lake Forest

14

Little boys growing up in the 1950s could ask Santa for a train set.

inconspicuously insert the sounds of a harp in between Christmas songs to remind the workers of these values.

One of the most enduring symbols of Christmas at Field's was the Great Tree, a yearly feature that began in 1907 in the Walnut Room. For many years, the store used a real tree, cut down from tall pine forests in northern Wisconsin or Minnesota and transported by flatbed railroad car to Chicago. A professional lumberman would select a perfect balsam at least seventy feet high, carefully remove just the top fifty feet or so, bind the branches carefully and load it on a sled to the train station. When the tree arrived in Chicago, it was transferred to a tractor trailer and brought to the store on a Saturday night.

In order to get the behemoth into the store, police would have to block traffic from the street while workmen removed the revolving doors and

A Marshall Field's Christmas box under the tree always caused excitement and anticipation. *Courtesy of Susan Greene.*

carefully eased the tree into the building. It was then hoisted up through the seven-story light well by block and tackle and moved carefully through the atrium into the Walnut Room, where it rested in a sturdy base that had been constructed in the central pond. Workmen would build a scaffolding around the tree and spend the rest of the night unbinding and straightening the branches and precisely placing up to 1,500 handmade decorations according to pre-drawn plans.

Due to the extreme fire danger posed by a fifty-foot live tree, workers also installed a specially designed chemical fire extinguishing system, which would be hidden in the tree's interior. Should a fire occur, the system could be triggered to smother the flames. In addition, firemen in rotating shifts stood by twenty-four hours a day to ensure the safety of

In its early years, the Great Tree was real, cut from northern balsam forests.

the store and its guests. None of that was obvious to shoppers, especially the children, who would gawk in open-mouthed delight at the monolith covered with huge, brightly colored ornaments, outsized strings of tinsel and gigantic icicles. Lunch under the tree in the Walnut Room became a cherished tradition for generations.

By the 1960s, the risk and expense of a real tree was too much to bear, and Field's contracted Colonial Decorative Display of New York to build a suitable artificial tree, which is still in use today. Some of the branches of the artificial balsam are over fifteen feet long and weigh as much as fifty pounds. The Great Tree remains the most enduring Christmas symbol at the store, and speculation among the public regarding each year's theme usually begins in early autumn.

Above: Lunch under the Great Tree was a Christmas tradition for Chicagoans. *Courtesy of Susan Greene.*

Right: In 2005, the Christmas campaign proclaimed, "There's no place like Field's at Christmas!" *Courtesy of Gloria Evenson.*

1960s Christmas under the dome featured sparkling white balloons. *Courtesy of Susan Greene.*

Of course, the Great Tree wasn't the only attraction at Christmastime. Field's vast toy department on the fourth floor magically transformed into Candy Cane Lane, with massive candy canes and other fanciful decorations flanking each aisle. There were toys of every description, from all corners of the globe. Dolls and trains and stuffed animals and books and puzzles and toy soldiers…everything that could be imagined, and more. For a child of the mid-twentieth century, it was simply too much to take in, and youngsters often fluctuated from glassy-eyed stares to screaming tantrums as their parents struggled to drag them by their heavy coats through the rows of goodies.

After a reconnaisance of Candy Cane Lane, it was time to ascend to the eighth floor, where Santa Claus lived. In the mid-1940s, Field's execs were casting about for something to differentiate Field's Santa from all the other Santas on State Street. In 1939, competitor Montgomery Ward had created Rudolph the red-nosed reindeer to pull Santa's sleigh, and the mythical beast had become a sensation. Field's display department needed a Rudolph of its very own.

Johanna Osbourne, a longtime Field's display employee, began kicking around the idea with her husband Addis, who was a teacher at the Art Institute of Chicago. Johanna envisioned a character that was a blend of her favorite jolly uncle and a Charles Dickens Christmas character. After some preliminary sketches, Uncle Mistletoe was introduced to the public in 1946. A portly little man with a warm smile and bushy black eyebrows, Uncle Mistletoe was Santa's "ambassador." He was decked out in a red frock coat, long white scarf and black top hat and boots. A sprig of mistletoe decorated his hat. Gauzy white wings allowed him to fly about like bumblebee, and he could almost always be found perched at the top of the Great Tree.

Uncle Mistletoe rivaled Santa in popularity among Chicago children. *Photo by Peter Rimsa.*

Christmas windows always portrayed a story. *Courtesy of Susan Pinto.*

Window detail, circa 1960. *Courtesy of Susan Pinto.*

Uncle Mistletoe's job was to manage the elves and assist Santa in identifying all the good little girls and boys. Kindness was an important trait to Santa, and Uncle Mistletoe soon headed up a Kindness Club, which issued an honorary Kindness Club button to well-behaved children, or at least those who took a pledge of good behavior. In 1948, fearing Uncle Mistletoe might become lonely in those long months between Christmases, Field's introduced Aunt Holly. Aunt Holly was an archetypal grandmother figure, wearing a red dress with starched white collar and apron, her gray hair done up in a bun circled with holly. A pair of wire-rimmed reading glasses perched on the tip of her nose, and her face was always wreathed in a kindly smile. Aunt Holly and Uncle Mistletoe lived in the Cozy Cloud Cottage on Field's eighth floor, where Aunt Holly baked cookies as Uncle Mistletoe scurried about making notes and assisting Santa.

The characters were a success beyond anyone's wildest dreams, and soon Santa was rather lonely at Field's, speaking to the occasional stray child, as lines formed to enter the Cozy Cloud Cottage of Uncle Mistletoe instead. Field's later added other characters to the mix, including Freddie Field Mouse and his family, Tony Pony, Otto the Elephant, elves Olio, Molio and Rolio, Aunt Judy, Skippy Monkey, Michael O'Hare and Obediah pig. Soon,

Santa coming down the chimney in a window display. *Courtesy of Susan Pinto.*

Cinderella Christmas windows were popular with little girls. *Courtesy of Gloria Evenson.*

the characters were so popular they sparked a year-round television show that lasted into the early 1950s. Actor Johnny Coons starred as the voice of Uncle Mistletoe, and Jennifer Holt, a former actress in television westerns, appeared as Aunt Judy, the only human in the cast of characters. The series spawned a huge amount of licensed goods, including records, puppets, dolls and a Golden Book.

Of course, not all the action was inside the store. The outside display windows, which were fabulous year round, took on a special sparkle during the holidays. In 1944, Field's team decided to use all thirteen of the display windows to tell a continuous story. They chose Clement Moore's epic poem, "A Visit from St. Nicholas": "'Twas the night before Christmas..." The windows each depicted a scene from the poem, with the text carefully displayed in a fanciful storybook placed at the window's base. Over 250,000 people passed by the windows each day, entranced by the story unfolding in front of their eyes. It was such a success that Field's repeated it in 1945.

In 1946, the theme "A Christmas Dream" introduced Uncle Mistletoe. In this story, a little boy named Jim-Jam and his sister Joann fall asleep and have a fabulous dream, in which Uncle Mistletoe comes through their window and whisks them away on a magic flying carpet for a visit with Santa at the North Pole. In recent years, the windows have reflected such themes as Charlie and the Chocolate Factory, Harry Potter, Cinderella and various Disney stories.

Although beautiful, none will ever match the wonderment of those from a simpler time, when ambassadors could fly and being kind to others was the only thing that really mattered.

Chapter 9

WINDS OF CHANGE

BATUS and Target

A man with a surplus can control circumstances, but a man without a surplus is controlled by them, and often has no opportunity to exercise judgment.

In 1977, Angelo R. Arena was hired as president of Marshall Field's, lured away from his position as head of Dallas-based Neiman Marcus, a division of Carter Hawley Hale. Arena was an outsider, but the board felt he had the talent to turn the company into a national chain. For many years, his old employer, Carter Hawley Hale, had wanted to acquire Field's, and in December of that year they offered a bid of $325 million. Although it was a good offer, Field's turned it down, wanting to keep the chain independent.

Arena moved forward with the expansion plans, and by 1981, Marshall Field's owned a total of ninety-three stores, although only nineteen were operating under the Field's banner. By the end of fiscal 1981, gross revenue topped $1 billion, but profits were disappointing. It seemed they had expanded too quickly and into too many markets, perhaps forgetting the founder's guiding principles that had carried them over one hundred years. Stock prices lagged, the company was ripe for a hostile takeover and the board of directors knew it.

Sure enough, in early 1982, the wolf was at the door in the form of corporate raider Carl Icahn. Icahn began to buy up large chunks of company stock, eventually accumulating a 30 percent share. The board realized that

The main aisle of State Street during the late 1960s. *Courtesy of Susan Greene.*

its days as an independent store were numbered, but it didn't want to fall into the raider's clutches. Members of the board immediately began to search for a gentler master, initiating talks with May Department Stores, Dayton-Hudson and even returning to Carter Hawley Hale. In 1982, the U.S. division of British tobacco giant BAT Industries PLC, or BATUS for short, stepped in and bought Marshall Field's for $367.6 million, or about $30 per share.

BATUS had a fair track record with American department stores, owning moderate to high-end retailers such as Saks Fifth Avenue and Gimbels. Its first move was to dismantle most of the acquisitions

Millinery Department, featuring designs by Schiaparelli. *Courtesy of Susan Greene.*

accomplished by Arena, spinning off or closing underperforming stores. Field's picked up five more Wisconsin stores that were previously Gimbels but then closed two a few years later. It opened a new store in Columbus, Ohio, and added a second store in Houston and one in San Antonio. By the time the dust settled in 1990, there were twenty-four stores operating under the Field's name: fifteen in Illinois, four in Wisconsin, four in Texas and one in Ohio.

Back in Chicago, the State Street store returned its attention to the principles of quality and service that had always guided it successfully in the past. Philip B. Miller, who had previously served as president of Neiman Marcus, joined as the new CEO and focused on attracting a younger and more upscale customer, adding new designer lines that included Bottega Veneta, Louis Vuitton, Fendi, Gucci and Chanel.

In 1987, BATUS began a $115 million renovation of the State Street Store. In the center of the store, an eleven-story glass-covered atrium and elaborate central fountain joined the State and Wabash halves of the first floor, which had previously been separated by a small service alley. The bargain basement, which had been an enduring feature since Harry Selfridge's days, gave way to a vast food court and small boutiques. The

Lingerie bags in luxurious colors and fabrics, circa 1968. *Courtesy of Susan Greene.*

changes paid off; in 1989, Field's reported gross sales of $1.09 billion and strong pretax profits of nearly $91 million.

Now that the stores were back on firm footing, some of the potential buyers that had turned their noses up during Icahn's attack decided to come back for another look. Once again, there was another hostile takeover bid, this time by an investor group headed by financier James Goldsmith. Ironically, one of the members was Ted Field, the great-great-grandson of Marshall the first. As BATUS struggled to fight off the $21.7 billion leveraged buyout, it divested itself of all its U.S. retail holdings. Dayton-Hudson Corporation stepped into the fray and purchased the Field's chain for $1.04 billion in June 1990. Dayton-Hudson was named for its Dayton Stores in Minneapolis and its Hudson Stores in Detroit, but its real cash cow was the rapidly expanding upscale discounter Target Stores.

Shortly after the takeover, Dayton-Hudson enraged some of its home markets by renaming several of the Dayton's and Hudson's stores as Marshall Field's. It was truly a compliment to Marshall Field's, because the new corporate owner obviously understood and appreciated the Field's brand cache, but generations of Detroit and Minneapolis folks were upset about losing their hometown brand identity. In 2000, the firm took the even more radical step of changing its corporate name to Target Corporation. In an effort to limit the brand splintering that had already occurred, Target then changed the name of all department stores under its command (except for its West Coast Mervyn's chain) to Marshall Field's. Thus, the company now had two easily identifiable and separately branded divisions: Target discount stores and Marshall Field's department stores.

In the beginning, Dayton-Hudson made several well-meaning but misguided changes in the Field's stores. It believed that the modern consumer was always price conscious, and it dropped some of the more prestigious brands in favor of less expensive merchandise. Consumers grumbled, and sales slowed. Then, in an innocuous move to trim costs, it replaced the heavy dark green Field's shopping bags with a good quality but rather plain brown Kraft bag. Somehow, this touched a nerve with loyal Field's shoppers, who began to howl so loudly and persistently that Dayton-Hudson had to actually take out advertisements apologizing for its misdeed while scrambling to restock the hallowed green bags.

If this tempest in a teapot sounds silly, it did serve to teach the corporation a lesson in tampering with brand loyalty, and by the Target days, the company was focused on restoring Field's once again to its past glory. Target quickly began to add more upscale lines, small boutiques and trendy items to the stores. It undertook another renovation of the State Street store in 2002 and began experimenting with the "store within a store" concept, opening a variety of high-end leased vendor departments such as Thomas Pink, Mimi Maternity, Wrigleyville Sports and Creative Kidstuff.

Just when it seemed that Field's had found a suitable corporate caretaker, trouble struck once more. Although Field's sales were healthy and holding their own in a difficult economy, Target's sales had grown so rapidly that the department store sector was an almost insignificant blip on its balance sheet. Under extreme and growing pressure from its investors and Wall Street wags, Target reluctantly agreed to divest itself of the department stores. The two most likely buyers were May Department Stores and Federated Department Stores, owner of Macy's. Analysts predicted the sale would generate about

Left: The famous Field's clock is replicated in many forms, including desk clocks, cookie jars and lamps. *Photo by Peter Rimsa.*

Below: Dept. 56, the manufacturer of Christmas villages and collectibles, honored Field's and Frangos in 2005 with a Frango Factory and Frango Delivery Van. *Photo by Peter Rimsa.*

The breathtaking Tiffany dome at Christmas 2005. *Courtesy of Gloria Evenson.*

The Great Tree in the Walnut Room during Marshall Field's last Christmas, 2005. *Courtesy of Gloria Evenson.*

$1.8 billion, but Federated and May both showed interest in the chain, driving up the eventual purchase price to an astronomical $3.2 billion.

May won the battle but lost the war. Overextended from the purchase, May owned the stores for less than one year before it fell prey to a takeover by Federated. During that year, Field's customers watched as May seemed on track to return the store to its roots. Its final Christmas theme was "There's no place like Field's," and it evoked memories of the best of Field's past. Unfortunately, by the following year, there would be no more Field's at all.

Chapter 10

AN ICON VANISHES

The Coming of Macy's

Good will is the one and only asset that competition cannot undersell or destroy.

In February 2005, less than one year after Field's was purchased by May Department Stores, Federated Department Stores, the corporate owner of Macy's, announced it would acquire May and all its holdings for $11 billion in cash and stock. It also agreed to assume $6 billion in May debt, bringing the total purchase price to around $17 billion. Marshall Field's was now in the hands of its third corporate owner in a little over one year's time.

At first, Chicago customers weren't too concerned. Actually, unless they'd lived or traveled extensively on the East Coast, most had little familiarity with Macy's at all. To Chicagoans, Macy's was a New York store that held a Thanksgiving Parade and mistreated Santa in *Miracle on 34th Street*.

Macy's was founded in New York City in 1858 by Rowland Hussey Macy. The store's characteristic red star logo was derived from a tattoo that Macy had gotten during his teenage years, when he worked on a Nantucket whaling ship. He died in 1877, but the store carrying his name lived on. The company underwent a large expansion campaign during the mid-1900s, opening and acquiring stores as far away as California. In 1988, the firm was purchased by Campeau Corporation, a Canadian real estate developer and investment firm. After another round of acquisitions, mergers and divestitures, the company filed for banruptcy protection in 1992.

In 1994, Federated began to woo Macy's with the intent to merge. Federated was an Ohio-based department store holding firm with a portfolio that included Abraham & Straus, Filene's and I. Magnin. Following the merger, Macy's moved its headquarters to Federated's Cincinnati offices.

After the 2005 purchase of May by Federated, rumblings began in the press that Terry Lundgren, Federated's CEO, chairman of the board, president and director, planned to rename the former May brands Macy's. Nervous ripples spread through Chicago, but most residents didn't believe that the name change would apply to Marshall Field's, the grande old dame whose name was practically synonymous with the city. Still, to be on the safe side, a petition started circulating under the web domain KeepItFields.org. Tens of thousands of people signed, some from as far away as Europe and Japan. Eventually, about sixty thousand people signed, including notables such as former Illinois governor James Thompson and Minnesota senator Dayton, a descendant of the family who founded Dayton stores.

The petition garnered a lot of press, but still the rumors persisted. Mr. Lundgren claimed that Federated had conducted a focus group and the analysis showed that most people were either indifferent to the name change or preferred the Macy's brand. Some folks pressed for details on the survey, such as who had performed it, what questions were included and which demographic was polled, but those facts were never released to the public or the media.

As time wore on, the rancor between Federated and many Chicago residents grew. Another grassroots group, FieldsFansChicago.org, began pleading the case for retaining the brand, but it fell on deaf ears. Federated, citing cost savings and the benefits of brand uniformity, announced that it would be renaming more than 400 former May stores under the Macy's label, giving the company a total of approximately 950 stores. One immediate result of the rebranding was that about 80 shopping malls nationwide suddenly found themselves with two Macy's stores as anchors.

In Chicago, things got ugly. On September 9, 2006, when the name officially changed, more than three hundred protestors carrying Chicago flags and "boycott Macy's" picket signs ringed the block around the State Street store. Chicago television and radio stations arrived on the scene as tour buses, taxicabs and even police cars honked in support. Chicago celebrities such as Roger Ebert, Oprah, WFMT Radio's Andrew Patner and *Chicago Tribune* columnist Ellen Warren weighed in, denouncing the name change or expressing disappointment.

Protestors in period dress shouted, "Give the lady what she wants!" at a 2007 rally. *Courtesy of Gloria Evenson.*

Marchers in front of State Street, 2008. *Courtesy of Gloria Evenson.*

Protestors hold up a sign for passing cars, 2009. *Courtesy of Gloria Evenson.*

Macy's executives assured the media that it was simply an emotional response and things would be back to normal before Christmas. Instead, the busy holiday season brought another protest, with protestors handing out leaflets, bumper stickers and buttons. Since 2006, protests and leafletting have continued unabated up through the present day.

Federated Department Stores announced in 2007 that it would ask shareholders to allow a change of the corporation's name to Macy's Inc. The change was approved and became official on June 1, 2007. Meanwhile, after facing a steadily declining economy and dwindling sales in many of the May doors, Macy's abandoned its "one size fits all" program of uniformity, which resulted in mittens and gloves in Florida stores during winter and other such anomolies.

Its new approach, "My Macy's," returns to the regionalized approach of tweaking buying for each market, although most of its offices have been consolidated into a central New York location. Recently, it signed exclusive agreements with various designers and celebrities such as Tommy Hilfiger, Madonna, Martha Stewart and Donald Trump. Its online business continues to grow, increasing by 29 percent in 2008, according to *Internet Retailer*, but

The cornerstone at Wabash and Washington. *Photo by Peter Rimsa.*

same-store sales in that year reportedly fell 7 percent as the country headed into an economic decline.

What all this means for the future of the once-great Chicago institution is unclear. Macy's execs have repeatedly claimed in the media that they don't break out individual store sales so they can't tell how the State Street store is doing in relation to others in the division.

One thing is certain: the landmark building with its towering marble columns, Tiffany mosaic dome and twin great clocks has represented the best of Chicago for over 100 years and will serve as a constant reminder of the young New England farm boy who came to this city more than 150 years ago spreading his message of honesty, fairness and hard work.

Epilogue

STATE STREET TODAY

There was no guarantee at that time that the place would ever become the western metropolis. The town had plenty of ambition and pluck; but the possibilities of greatness were hardly visible.

State Street today bears little resemblance to the shopping district of Field and Palmer's era. Gone are almost all of the original department stores that lured the city's ladies to a delightful day of shopping. Most of them, including the Fair, Mandel Brothers, Schlesinger and Mayer, Goldblatt's and Wieboldt's simply disappeared over time, victims of poor economies, poor management or corporate mergers. Montgomery Ward's, which began as a mail-order house, closed its retail stores in 2001 and returned to its mail-order roots.

Carson Pirie Scott and Company still exists today as part of the Bon-Ton Stores, but the firm was forced to abandon its flagship Louis Sullivan store on State Street and retreat to the suburbs in 2007 when the aging building required extensive renovations. Now renamed the Sullivan Building in honor of its architect, it's being redeveloped as a mixed-use retail hub, with rumored future tenants including Target Corp., ironically one of the past owners of Marshall Field's, and possibly a high-end grocery store.

Sears still maintains a store on State at Madison Street that opened in 1986. Ironically, the original Sears State Street flagship store, which opened in 1932, flourished for fifty-four years at State and Congress in a now-historic building constructed in 1891 by Field's old partner, Levi Z. Leiter. The building is now a campus for Robert Morris University. In 1995, the company was forced, after years of economic decline, to give up its namesake Sears Tower (now renamed Willis Tower) at 233 South Wacker, once the tallest building in the world and, as of this writing, still the tallest building in America. It could lose that distinction to another Chicago building, the Spire, which is planned to top out at two thousand feet. Unfortunately, the tumbling economy and various other problems have stalled the project, and its future is uncertain.

The stately Marshall Field store continues to grace State Street. The building was granted status as a National Historic Landmark in 1978, and in 2005, the City of Chicago also bestowed landmark status upon it in an effort to protect it from significant changes under new ownership. The brass plaques on the side of the building read "Marshall Field and

The Great Clock has always been a meeting place for Chicagoans. *Courtesy of Gloria Evenson.*

Company," but the trademark green awnings are gone, replaced by black ones bearing the Macy's name. Macy's originally intended to install large lighted signs on the building but abandoned the idea after local preservationists threatened lawsuits.

Today, most of the businesses on State Street are national specialty chains such as Old Navy and the Gap or "off-price" outlets, including Filene's Basement and Loehmann's. Higher-end retailers such as Neiman Marcus, Saks Fifth Avenue and Nordstrom have mostly migrated to Michigan Avenue, the Chicago shopping district known as the "magnificent mile." Marshall Field's also had a store there, which was taken over by Macy's.

Most of the customers arrive today by bus, car or bicycle instead of elegant horse drawn carriages of yesteryear. Today's gentle lady is likely to be clothed in jeans or perhaps a business suit, in contrast to the bustles and crinolines of yore. The plank highways are a distant memory, replaced by high-speed concrete interstates that crisscross the country. Jet airplanes soar overhead, making global travel much easier and faster than the mere cross-country train trips of the early twentieth century. The streets are no longer muddy or rutted, but homeless still beg for change on the corners. Today, like in Field's day, the city remains a mix of great wealth and wretched poverty. Much has changed, but surprisingly, much remains the same since that fateful day when young Marshall Field stepped off the train and into the chaos of early Chicago.

One thing, however, is certain: the city and its culture would be much poorer today had it not been graced by its association with the world's greatest merchant and the ideals and generosity he bestowed upon it.

Appendix

Marshall Field's Recipes

There is no happiness in mere dollars…it is given a man to eat so much…and more he cannot use.

Although almost everything Marshall Field did was the result of careful thought and long-range planning, the store's legendary restaurants and tearooms arose in response to a simple and serendipitous event. In early 1890, a millinery clerk named Mrs. Sarah Hering was assisting a pair of lady shoppers in her department. As they examined the fine merchandise, one woman complained of feeling unwell, as she had not eaten all day. State Street in 1890 had few establishments that were considered suitable for an unescorted woman, so the shoppers of the day would have to return home to enjoy a meal.

Perhaps feeling sorry for the customer, or perhaps unwilling to lose a large sale, Mrs. Hering pulled out a small table and chairs and invited the women to sit down and eat the lunch she had prepared for herself, a chicken potpie. The women were delighted and thought the potpie was superb. As the story goes, they excitedly asked if she would allow them to return the next day with some of their well-to-do friends. Mrs. Hering agreed, and the following afternoon, armed with potpies she had baked at home, the innovative millinery clerk set up five tables in the back of her department and hosted an impromptu luncheon. Other reports claim that Mrs. Hering was involved

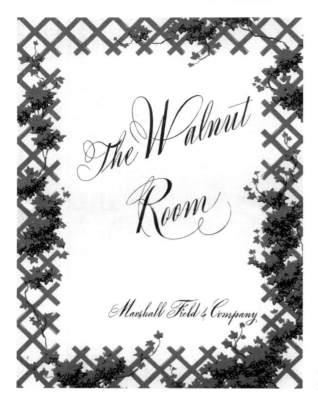

Cover of Walnut Room
menu from 1942.

in merchandising or marketing for the store and did not actually serve guests but merely suggested the idea of restaurants. One thing is certain—her signature potpie is still a hit, over one hundred years later.

Harry Selfridge, a young manager who would later go on to open the iconic Selfridge's of London, immediately realized the genius of in-store restaurants. By offering food and beverages to the customers, they would remain in the store longer, perhaps spending more money. He approached Field with the idea, and the South Tea Room opened on the third floor of the State Street store in April 1890. On opening day, it had fifteen tables (each adorned with a red rose), eight waitresses and four cooks. Fifty-six guests lunched that day on corned beef hash, Mrs. Hering's potpies, chicken salad and orange punch served in an orange shell. At the end of the first year, over 1,500 meals were served each day, and by 1920, Marshall Field's State Street store had a total of seven restaurants, grills and tearooms throughout the store. Since that time, Mrs. Hering's famous chicken potpie has become synonymous with dining at Field's.

Field's Famous Foods

1—Field's New England Salt Pork, Fried Country Style and served with
Cream Gravy, Baked Idaho Potato, Spiced Crabapple, Philadelphia Relish . . 65

2—Field's Tea Room Parfait 30

3—Field's Special Sandwich (Sliced Breast of Chicken, Swiss Cheese, Tomato,
Thousand Island Dressing, Crisp Bacon, Ripe Olive), Coffee or Tea 75

Special Luncheons

Cream of Corn Soup   Vegetable Cocktail

40—Yankee Pot Roast, Whipped Potatoes and Carrot Circles 1.00

41—Chicken and Vegetables en Casserole with Fluffy Whipped Potato Top and
Tossed Combination Salad, Field's French Dressing 1.15

42—Homemade Meat Balls with Italian Spaghetti, Garden Green Beans 90

43—A Plate of Assorted Cold Cuts and Cheese, Field's Potato Salad and Tomato Slices 95

44—Steamed Finnan Haddie, Drawn Butter, Carrot Circles and
Garden Green Beans 90

46—Vegetable Plate: Whipped Potatoes, Garden Green Beans, Carrot Circles and Tomato Slices . 85

Homemade Apple Pie   Cherry Pie
Burnt Sugar Layer Cake, Caramel Icing   Chocolate Nut Pudding
Royal Anne Cherries, Cookie   Camembert Cheese with Salted Crackers
Choice of Ice Cream or Sherbet   Half a Chilled Grapefruit

Coffee or Tea

No Substitutions, please

All prices are our ceiling prices or below. By O. P. A. regulations our ceilings are based on our highest prices from April
4th to April 10th, 1943. Our menus or price lists for that week are available for your inspection.

In 1942, a full lunch at the Walnut Room cost about one dollar.

MRS. HERING'S FAMOUS ORIGINAL CHICKEN POTPIE

Pie Dough:
1½ cups flour, sifted
½ tsp. salt
8 tbsp. (1 stick) cold unsalted butter, cut into small pieces
¼ cup vegetable shortening (Crisco), chilled
3–4 tbsp. ice water

Chicken:
1 frying chicken, approx. 3 lbs.
1 carrot

1 celery stalk
1 small onion, halved
2 tsp. salt

Filling:
6 tbsp. unsalted butter
1 large onion, diced (about 1¼ cups)
3 carrots, thinly sliced on the diagonal
3 celery stalks, thinly sliced on the diagonal
½ cup flour
1½ cups milk
1 tsp. chopped fresh thyme leaves
¼ cup sherry
¾ cup frozen green peas, thawed
2 tbsp. fresh minced parsley
2 tsp. salt
½ tsp. freshly ground black pepper
1 egg whisked with 1 tbsp. water for glazing

To prepare pie dough:
Combine flour, salt and butter in the bowl of a food processor and pulse five times to combine. Add the shortening and pulse a few more times, until the dough resembles coarse cornmeal. Transfer to a bowl and sprinkle with 3 tbsp. ice water. Stir and then press together to form a ball. If the dough won't come together, add more water as needed. Flatten the dough into a disk. Cover in plastic wrap and refrigerate for at least thirty minutes or up to two days before rolling.

To cook chicken:
Combine chicken, carrot, celery, onion and salt in a large stockpot. Add cold water as needed to cover and bring to a boil over high heat. Decrease the heat to low and simmer for forty-five minutes. Remove chicken, reserving liquid, and transfer chicken to a plate and allow it to cool. Increase the heat to high and boil the remaining broth for twenty minutes to reduce and concentrate. Strain the broth through a fine-mesh sieve and discard the vegetables. Reserve broth. When cool enough to handle, pull the chicken meat from the bones and shred into bite-size pieces.

To prepare filling:

Place a large saucepan over medium heat and add butter. When the butter is melted, add the onion, carrots and celery and cook, stirring occasionally for ten minutes, until the onion is soft and translucent. Add the flour and cook, stirring constantly, for one minute. Slowly whisk in the milk and 2½ cups of reserved chicken broth. Decrease the heat to low and simmer, stirring often, for ten minutes. Add the chicken meat, thyme, sherry, peas, parsley, salt and pepper and stir well. Taste and adjust seasoning as necessary. Divide the filling among six twelve-ounce potpie tins or individual ramekins.

To assemble and bake:

Preheat oven to 400 degrees Fahrenheit. Next, place chilled dough on a floured surface and roll out to ¼-inch thick. Cut into six rounds about 1 inch larger than the circumference of the tins or ramekins. Carefully place a dough round over each filled dish. Turn the edges of the dough back under itself and flute the edges with a fork. Cut a 1-inch slit in the top of each pie. Brush the dough with the egg and water mixture to glaze and seal the top, which will give the final product an attractive finish. Line a baking sheet

Spice Island recipe booklet, 1952.

SPICE
ISLANDS
RECIPES
for

Curry · Saffron

Vanilla Beans

Mei Yen
Seasoning Powder

Arrowroot

Horseradish

Herb Butters

Gourmet Sauces

SPICE ISLANDS
COMPANY
SAN FRANCISCO 7
CALIFORNIA

SOLD BY
THE PANTRY - SEVENTH FLOOR
MIDDLE STATE

Marshall Field & Company
CHICAGO - 90 - ILLINOIS

The seventh-floor Pantry sold food items,
including spices and condiments.

with foil to catch the liquid that will bubble over and place pies on baking sheet and bake for twenty-five minutes or until the pastry is golden and the filling bubbles. Serve hot. Makes six individual pies or one large potpie.

MRS. HERING'S QUICK CHICKEN POTPIE (EASY VERSION)

1 sheet frozen puff pastry dough, thawed
3 tbsp. chicken fat or butter
¼ cup flour
2 cups chicken broth
salt and pepper to taste
12-ounce package cooked chicken breast meat, cut or torn into bite-sized strips
¼ cup petite frozen peas, thawed
¼ cup diced cooked carrots
½ tsp. dried thyme

Directions:

Preheat oven to 450 degrees Fahrenheit. Using potpie tins or individual ramekins, cut circles from the puff pastry to slightly overlap the tops of the dishes. Melt fat or butter in a medium pan and add flour, stirring constantly for about a minute. Add broth, whisking until smooth. Heat to a boil and cook one to two minutes until thickened. Season with salt and pepper to taste. Add cooked chicken, peas, carrots and thyme. Heat through and then divide the mixture among the ramekins. Top with a pastry round, tuck the edges in and flute with fork. Cut a one-inch slit in each pie to vent. Place on foil-lined baking sheet and bake twenty to twenty-five minutes until puffy and golden. Serve hot. Makes two individual pies.

MARSHALL FIELD'S CHICKEN SALAD

Homemade Mayonnaise:
1 whole egg (use pasteurized egg due to risks of consuming uncooked eggs)
1 tsp. Dijon mustard
¼ tsp. salt
1½ cups canola oil
1½ tbsp. fresh lemon juice
pinch of white pepper to taste
pinch of cayenne pepper to taste

Chicken Salad Dressing:
½ cup Homemade Mayonnaise (recipe above)
¼ cup sour cream
1 heaping tbsp. Dijon mustard
1 tsp. granulated sugar
¼ tsp. salt
¼ tsp. white pepper, or more to taste
2½ tsp. fresh lemon juice

Chicken Salad:
1½ cups shredded cooked chicken
½ cup celery, finely chopped
2 tbsp. green onions (scallions), finely chopped
¼ cup pecans, toasted, chopped
½ cup halved seedless green grapes
1 recipe Chicken Salad Dressing (recipe above)

Homemade Mayonnaise:
In a food processor, blend whole egg, Dijon mustard and salt. Process together for one minute. Add canola oil to running processor in slow, steady stream. Continue to run for at least one minute beyond when the mixture is completely emulsified. Add lemon juice, a pinch of white pepper and cayenne. Process briefly to mix. Refrigerate.

Chicken Salad Dressing:
Combine mayonnaise, sour cream, Dijon mustard, sugar, salt, white pepper and lemon juice, and mix well.

Chicken Salad:
Combine chicken, celery, scallions, pecans, grapes and dressing. Mix well and refrigerate at least two hours.

MARSHALL FIELD'S CHICKEN SALAD SANDWICH

For each sandwich:
1 thick slice sweet whole-grain bread
½ cup Marshall Field's Chicken Salad (recipe above)
3 slices bacon, cooked crisp
1 thick slice provolone or white cheddar

Cover bread with the chicken salad. Place under broiler for about a minute, till heated but not bubbly. Remove and place bacon and cheese on top. Return to broiler and melt cheese. Serve immediately.

IMITATION FRANGO MINTS

Real Frango mints are made from a closely guarded secret recipe, but this copycat recipe approximates the taste, if not the texture and creaminess of the authentic treats.

18 ounces semisweet chocolate chips
1 tbsp. mint extract
1 cup unsalted butter
2 cups powdered (confectioner's) sugar
2 whole eggs (pasteurized)

Melt chocolate chips over low heat in a double boiler. Allow chocolate to cool slightly, add the remaining ingredients and beat until well combined. Pour into a lightly greased pan and refrigerate until mixture begins to harden. Cut into cubes while still pliable. Keep refrigerated.

Field's cookbooks were always popular, and this commemorative edition included lots of favorite recipes. *Photo by Peter Rimsa.*

MARSHALL FIELD'S FRANGO MINT CHEESECAKE

Chocolate Cookie Crust:
1 cup chocolate wafer cookie crumbs (about 20 cookies). If using Oreo cookies, separate in half and scrape off and discard filling.
4 tbsp. melted unsalted butter
2 tbsp. granulated sugar

Mix ingredients thoroughly in a blender or food processor. Press the mixture firmly into the bottom of an ungreased spring form pan. Preheat oven to 350 degrees Fahrenheit.

Filling:
15 Frango original mint chocolates (approx. 5½ ounces if using imitation Frangos above)
1 cup granulated sugar

3 (8-ounce) packages cream cheese, softened at room temperature
2 whole eggs, room temperature
$\frac{1}{3}$ cup heavy whipping cream
$\frac{1}{2}$ tsp. pure vanilla extract

Melt the Frangos in a slow simmering double boiler, using caution not to overheat, which can cause the chocolate to break down and change texture. Stir frequently and remove from heat once melted and smooth. While the Frangos cool slightly, combine the sugar and cream cheese in a separate bowl and beat with an electric mixer at medium speed until blended. Add the eggs one at a time and blend thoroughly, scraping the sides of the bowl as needed. Add the melted Frangos, whipping cream and vanilla extract, and beat to combine thoroughly. Pour filling mixture on top of crust in spring form pan. Place on center oven rack and bake for approximately thirty-five minutes, until the sides rise and appear done. The center of the cake will appear under baked and slightly fluid, but it will firm up as it cools. Do not over bake or the resulting cake will be crumbly and dry. Cool completely before serving, and top with whipped cream if desired.

Marshall Field's Marketplace Deli Oriental Chicken Pasta Salad

Pasta Salad:
8 oz fusilli pasta, cooked and well drained
1 $\frac{1}{4}$ lbs. boneless, skinless chicken breast, cooked and cut into julienne strips
8 ounces fresh pea pods, blanched and halved lengthwise
$\frac{1}{2}$ cup chopped green onions (scallions)
1 $\frac{1}{2}$ cups thinly sliced mushrooms
1 cup sesame dressing (see recipe below)
kosher salt and freshly ground pepper, to taste
$\frac{1}{2}$ lb. wonton skins
11-ounce can mandarin oranges, drained

Sesame dressing:
1 egg yolk
$\frac{1}{4}$ cup soy sauce
$\frac{1}{4}$ cup vinegar

¼ cup granulated sugar
¼ tsp. white pepper or to taste
1 cup sesame oil
½ cup canola oil

For sesame dressing:
In heavy saucepan, combine egg yolk and soy sauce. Cook over very low heat, stirring constantly, until mixture reaches 160 degrees Fahrenheit on instant-read thermometer. Set pan in ice water and stir to cool quickly. (Note: if you are using pasteurized eggs, you can skip this step and simply beat together egg yolk and soy sauce.) In food processor or blender, combine yolk–soy sauce mixture, vinegar, sugar and white pepper. Blend completely. Slowly add oils, mixing until emulsified. If you prefer less intense sesame flavor, you can adjust the ratio of sesame and canola oil, as long as the oil total equals 1½ cups. Measure 1 cup for use in pasta salad. Refrigerate unused portion.

For pasta salad:
In large bowl, combine pasta, chicken, pea pods, scallions and mushrooms. Toss gently. Pour 1 cup sesame dressing over mixture and toss to coat. Add salt and white pepper to taste. Chill well.

Before serving, prepare wonton skins: Slice wonton skins into ¼-inch strips and fry in vegetable oil until crisp. They will brown in thirty to sixty seconds in 350-degree Fahrenheit oil. Drain strips on paper towel. Garnish salad with fried wonton strips and mandarin oranges. Makes six to eight servings.

BIBLIOGRAPHY

Ditchett, S.H. *Marshall Field and Company: The Life Story of a Great Concern*. New York: Dry Goods Economist, 1922.

Dystel, Oscar, ed. "Picture Story: Fabulous Field's." *Coronet Magazine*, April 1945.

Ledermann, Robert P. *Christmas on State Street 1940s and Beyond*. Chicago: Arcadia Publishing, 2002.

Marden, Orison Swett. "Marshall Field: Determination Not to Remain Poor Made a Farmer Boy a Merchant Prince." In *Little Visits with Great Americans or Success Ideals and How to Attain Them*, Part 1. Whitefish, MT: Kessinger Publishing, 2003 (reprint, 1901 interview).

Twyman, Robert W. *The History of Marshall Field and Company, 1852–1906*. Philadelphia: University of Pennsylvania Press, 1954.

Wendt, Lloyd, and Herman Kogan. *Give the Lady What She Wants*. South Bend, IN: And Books, 1952.

Visit us at
www.historypress.net